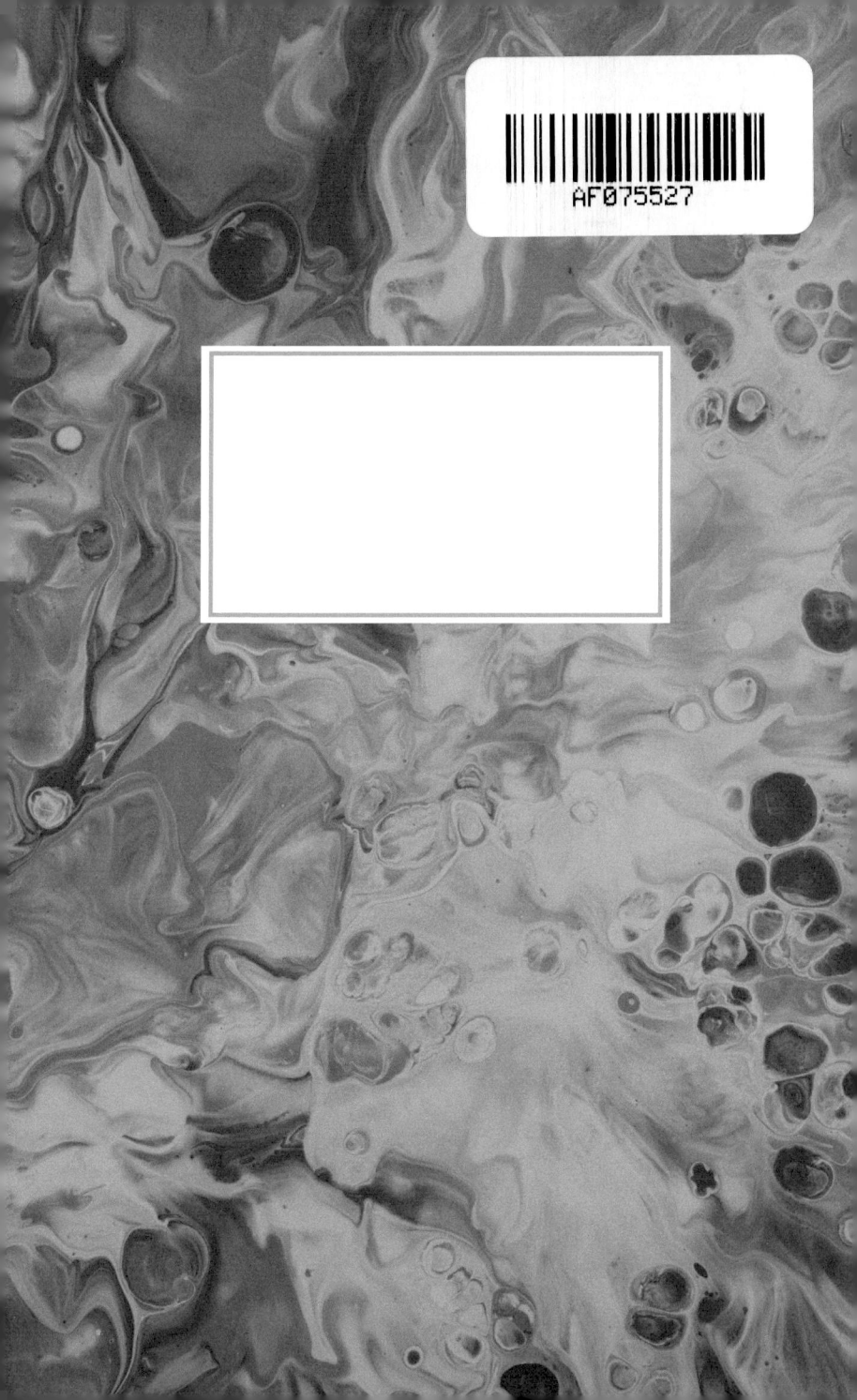

ANNE PIA was born in Edinburgh. The grandchild of Italian immigrants, she was raised surrounded by the culture, traditions, food and dialect of southern Italy. Her grandmother cooked the food of her native Viticuso: simple food using fresh seasonal produce with an emphasis on vegetables and grains – and feast day food, such as 18-egg frittatas for Easter Sunday mornings. Fresh ice cream churning, the hissing of a coffee machine and the latest Italian pop songs were the soundtrack to Anne's time in the family café – The Copper Kettle – in Bruntsfield. Throughout her life Anne has spent extensive periods in Italy living with Italian families and this has furthered her passion for and her ability to cook *la cucina povera*.

Anne's career as a writer has focused on identity, immigration, language, otherness and sexuality. Her first book, *Language of My Choosing*, was shortlisted for the Saltire Award for Best New Book of 2017. It was published in Italian in 2018 and later that year was awarded the Premio Flaiano Italianistica: La Cultura Italiana nel Mondo. Anne's subsequent books of poetry and essays have been well received and in 2022 she was invited to join the judging panel for the Scottish National Book Awards, a role she is undertaking again in 2023.

This is more than a cookery book. It is a glorious 'Te Deum' to Italy expressed through food, wine, music and anecdote. When you feel the 'nostalgia d'Italia' really badly and can't hop on a flight straight away, open this book, plunge in and all will be well.
RONNIE CONVERY, HONORARY ITALIAN CONSUL

With prose which demands to be read and recipes just begging to be cooked, all written with the style and poetic flair which we have come to expect from Anne Pia, Magnaccioni: My Food... My Italy *stands alongside the work of Diane Henry, Simon Hopkinson, and Nigel Slater – writers whose cookbooks you return to again and again.*
ALISTAIR BRAIDWOOD, SCOTS WHAY HAE!

By the same author:

Non-Fiction
Language of My Choosing (Luath Press, 2017)
Keeping Away the Spiders: Essays on Breaching Barriers (Luath Press, 2020)

Poetry
Transitory (Luath Press, 2018)
The Sweetness of Demons (Vagabond Voices, 2021)
Dragons Wear Lipstick (Dreich, 2022)

Magnaccioni

My Food... My Italy

ANNE PIA

Luath Press Limited
EDINBURGH
www.luath.co.uk

For Geraldine,
for her endless support and steadfast love.

First published 2023

ISBN 978-1-80425-124-9 hardback
ISBN: 978-1-80425-090-7 paperback

The author's right to be identified as author of this book
under the Copyright, Designs and Patents Act 1988 has been asserted.

The paper used in this book is recyclable. It is made from low
chlorine pulps produced in a low energy, low emission manner
from renewable forests.

Printed and bound by
Severn, Gloucester

Typeset in 10.5 point Sabon LT Pro by
Main Point Books, Edinburgh

Text and photographs © Anne Pia 2023

Contents

Introduction	11

A place to start

	27
fritto misto	30
sage oil	32

Antipasti… relaxing with guests

focaccia	40
piadine (Italian flatbreads)	43
PLATEFULS OF SUNSHINE	44
marinaded tomatoes (pomodori all'aglio)	45
tomato and onion salad (insalata di pomodori)	45
stuffed beef tomatoes (pomodori ripieni)	47
MUSHROOMS	48
mushrooms with lemons and walnuts	
(funghi con noci e limone)	51
CAULIFLOWER	52
cauliflower with olives and lemons	
(cavolfiore con olive e limone)	52
cauliflower with tuna (cavolfiore con tonno)	53
POTATO SALAD	53
simple potato salad (insalata di patate)	54
SMOKED HADDOCK	55
smoked haddock Italian style (pesce scozzese)	56

ARTICHOKES	57
sautéed artichokes with garlic and lemons (carciofi trifolati)	60
BROCCOLI AND BROCCOLETTI	61
broccoli fritters (frittelle di broccoli)	62
SALUMI (CURED MEATS)	62

Le frittate 65

a simple frittata (frittata di terra) for two	74
frittata with Savoy cabbage, onion and potato	
(la frittata con verza, cipollo e patate)	75
frittata with leftover pasta (frittata di pasta)	76
mozza frittata (frittata con mozzarella)	78
the Easter frittata (frittata pasqualina)	81

L'ora dell'aperitivo 83

traditional crostini (crostini semplici)	90

The best of life 91

SOME NOTES ON PREPARING PASTA	99
a basic beef sugo (ragù napoletano or ragù di manzo)	101
ragù di salsiccia	103
a light tomato sauce (sugo di pomodori freschi)	104
a medium to rich tomato sauce (sugo di pomodori)	105
the soffritto	106
trofie with pesto (trofie al pesto genovese)	108
trofie with potatoes and green beans	
trofie al pesto, con patate e fagiolini)	109

stuffed pasta shells (conchiglioni ripieni)	110
bolognese sauce	111
béchamel sauce	112
pasta and bean stew Viticuso style	
(pasta e fagiol' alla viticusar)	113
orzo with pesto and hazelnuts (orzo al pesto con nocciole)	115
spaghetti with a garlic and olive oil sauce	
(spaghetti all'aglio e olio)	116

La cucina povera 117

BRODO (BROTH OR STOCK)	121
vegetable stock	121
chicken stock	122
beef stock	122
pastina (small pasta for soup)	123
pastina in a broth (pastina in brodo)	124
stracciatella	124
PICCHIAPÒ	125
picchiapò	126
uova al sugo di pomodoro	127
a hearty soup (la minestra)	128
green minestrone (minestrone alla ligure)	129
pappa or pappocce'	130
RISOTTO	132
risotto with smoked haddock and peas	
(risotto di pesci e piselli)	134

risotto with mushrooms and black olives	
(risotto alla romana)	135
risotto with aubergines, basil and feta	137
(risotto alle melanzane con basilico e feta)	138
risotto with beetroot, mint and goats cheese	138
(risotto alla barbietola con formaggio di capra)	138
POLENTA	139
classic polenta (polenta al sugo di pomodoro)	141
scagliozzi (street food of the south)	142

Ports, boats and Marechiaro 143

fish soup (zuppa di pesci) 149

La cucina di terra 153

rough bread salad (panzanella)	157
BEANS, PULSES AND GREENS	158
Mariuccia's lentils (insalata di lenticchie)	158
chickpea salad with black olives, green beans and lemons	
(insalata di ceci con olive, fagioli e limone)	159
bean and tuna salad with capers	
(insalata di fagioli con tonno e caperi)	160
butter bean salad with rocket and beef tomatoes	
(fagioli bianchi con rucola e pomodoro)	160
bean stew (fagioli all'uccelletto)	161
butter bean casserole (fagioli bianchi al forno)	162
sautéed greens (cicoria, cavolo nero, spinaci ripassati)	163
roasted fennel (finocchio al forno)	163

brussels sprouts with pancetta
(cavoletti di Bruxelles o broccoletti con aglio e pancetta)   164
DRESSINGS   165
gremolata   166
pepperoncino   166
agrodolce   167
pangrattato   167

The sweet South   169

homemade ricotta (ricotta fresca)   160

A particular way of life   177

The food   181

The wine   183

The music   184

The language   186

Key to family collage   190

Acknowledgements   191

Introduction

Fiumicino airport

THE DISPLAY OF breads and bakes, of panini, fetching friselle, pane casareccio, pizze bianche (crisp and blistered and enough in themselves with just some salt); of Roman panatelle, fat, round and soft, topped with a light, golden crust, loaded and dripping, filled with a duo of folded, wafer-thin pancetta and guanciale, or salsiccia and caciocavallo cheese, sliced triangles of creamy, tangy goodness. Mozzarella in carrozza; a sandwich with hunks of mozzarella cheese, dipped in flour and milk then fried... glowing, crusty with melting cheese and mortadella focaccia with thick sliced provolone cheese wedges... all of these and more, at the counter of an airport café in Rome's Fiumicino airport, have me wide-eyed and spellbound. My appetite explodes; my insides growl. I want to eat everything. I am at a loss as to what to choose.

My choice for coffee is simple. Any one of the dozen or so coffees on offer will do. No debate here about whether or not it will be good. It's always good in Italy, even at airports. Indeed, it is particularly good at airports and railway stations, because Italians are always on the move and Italians need their coffee. Maybe I will have a caffè corretto with a little grappa added, to go with this one-time breakfast treat. Maybe I shouldn't, it is *only* 10.30 in the morning after all.

I sweep the area with my gaze. I love watching Italians eat. I see elegantly turned out women, all sunglasses and hair, bangled and strappy, trousered and bloused; professional men, proudly male, in dark suits with white, white shirts and carefully knotted ties. Despite their Roman *maniere*, and all the affectations of people who know they are seen, and indeed want to be, they are tucking into their food *con cuore* (with a voracity from the depths of them).

There is something unrestrainedly visceral about this. They bite hard, and – God Bless them for it – take huge mouthfuls, chew with vigour, savour every moment, talk at the same time, stop neither; and all in a context of refined, considered, stylish presentation. And I love these people.

Backstory and legend

As Letitia Clark comments in her book on the food of Sardinia, *Bitter Honey:* 'Recipe books are not just books of recipes. They are also chronicles of traditions, stories, and memories'.

I was born in Edinburgh, into a post-war immigrant Italian family and brought up by my Italian grandmother, Mariuccia (née Coletta). In 1913, she and my grandfather, Emilio Rossi travelled to Scotland from Viticuso, a small village in Lazio, southern Italy. They settled in the Bonnington area of Edinburgh. Through their warm friendly manner, hard work and a real will to make a life here, they earned the affection and respect of their Scottish neighbours. However, very soon after Italy declared war on Britain in WW2, my grandfather was arrested as an Italian national and together with around 700 other Italian men was loaded onto the ill-fated *Arandora Star*, a converted passenger liner, which left from Liverpool on 2 July 1940 bound for Canada. The unmarked boat was still in British waters when it was torpedoed by a passing German submarine. My grandfather drowned, along with his brother, Pietro Rossi and most of the other Prisoners of War, some as young as 16 years old. The whole event took a short half hour. The dying took longer.

Every Italian family in Scotland was affected. On top of their traditional domestic responsibilities of children and home – and in our case, helping in the family café – women were now forced to take charge of family businesses and become primary breadwinners. Most were unable to read and write even in their own language. An even greater challenge was that of rebuilding trust, regaining acceptance and respectability within a community which had largely turned against them. This they did through graciousness, generosity and their winning ways. Many of my Scottish friends speak with huge affection of the hospitality shown to them by their Italian neighbours. The door was always open and they were always given a place at the family table, always energetically encouraged to 'eat up'. Many saw themselves as part of these families. These strong, resilient women ensured through the values they passed on that their children and grandchildren had every opportunity to thrive, to deepen roots and to belong. As a community, we owe much to them.

Mariuccia (Grandma)

My creative memoir *Language of My Choosing* tells the story of the lifelong inspiration and influence of my grandma who was one of those women. Born almost ten years after she was widowed, I never cease to be amazed at her struggle and her determination to survive, at her wonderful belief, despite it all, in the generosity of the Scots and in human nature.

I grew up in and around the family café, The Copper Kettle, in Edinburgh's Bruntsfield. My mother took over the running of the business when I was six years old and my father had left. My grandmother looked after me from then until her death in 1964 when I was 14. My childhood memories are different to those of the Scottish girls I was at school with; they are of Grandma around the kitchen and a home life dominated by café opening hours. The Copper Kettle was usually open every day of the year, including Christmas and New Year, and stayed open until late at night. I have then, magical memories of fresh ice cream churning, of frothy coffees and a hissing coffee machine, and the Viennese, earth-dark coffee beans that made our café so popular.

Memories too of later, risky menu adventures, such as the brief departure from a menu with chips (always home cut!) to lemon sole cooked with muscatel raisins, and steak pizzaiuola (thin cuts poached in a rich tomato sauce).

I learned so much from Grandma. I clearly remember her careful tones in broken English, interspersed with choice words and old sayings in a Lazio dialect. I was in awe of her. She was fierce and energetic. Tenderness was less her way. Yet I loved her quaint mantras, her sage, old world wisdom and philosophy of life. I am reminded of her often and I am warmed by Italian friends on social media who articulate that same simple world view; speaking their truth and their joy in nature, outpouring their gratitude and deep respect for all that the land brings. Anna del Conte rightly tells us that Italians like to eat what they see growing. My Italian friends living in Roccasecca, Picinisco and Casalvieri put up canny shots of baskets overflowing with ripe kiwi and cherries, of courgettes freshly picked and preserved in jars, laid down for another season. They post photos of their olive groves, their orange trees ripe for the harvesting in carefully tended orchards. This for me is photographic poetry.

Grandma's survival in the hardest times came from her belief in the importance of fresh produce. Her diet and what we ate at home consisted mainly of vegetables and pulses. I can still see her quickening her pace in excitement at suddenly coming upon a delicately green, crunchy-leaved display of newly arrived frisée lettuces outside the local greengrocers. Rushing home with two in her bag, she first graced them with an olive oil and vinegar dressing... first the oil and then the vinegar. To this she added minced garlic and a chopped, hard-boiled egg. The taste of this salad with its eggy dressing was just delicious.

It was Grandma's values, the woman that she was through her personal journey of survival and my early years of being steeped in the rich simplicity of rural Italian cuisine, together with the spinning plates, the rock and roll, high octane years of café life, which underpin my lifelong affair with food and the kitchen.

Typically, women of her time and tradition were never wasteful. Grandma's repertoire of dishes was limited, based on few ingredients and even fewer cooking techniques. But she turned leftovers into feasts. Her sugo was quintessential. Her pizzas irreplaceable, the dough made with only two ingredients, flour and eggs... and only two ingredients for a topping... strips of tomato and golden, sizzling garlic; finished of course with olive oil. Tomatoes even in Scotland were plentiful but lacking the sweetness of the Mezzogiorno sun. To achieve the flavours she craved, she grew herbs, parsley and mint mainly, in a small patch of earth behind her Bruntsfield flat.

Living to eat

Magnaccioni: My Food... My Italy celebrates this precious cultural legacy. *Magnaccioni* is a Roman word meaning people 'who live to eat well', who seek plenty of good fare. In southern Italian homes *magnaccioni* are approved of, encouraged to eat and ask for more. I admit to still being seduced by these old ideas. If you like your food you are trustworthy, wholesome and genuine. You are vibrant, a lover of all that life offers, someone to be invited and enjoyed. Because of this cultural philosophy, no meal for me is a quickly put together, rustled up affair. Whether alone or with my partner and family every meal is planned as pleasure. Eating for me and for those around me is always something to look forward to. I am an enthusiastic home cook.

When you come to my home, I want you to be happy. And I show my love and appreciation of you through cooking for you. When my girls come home, when visitors come from afar, it is not unusual for me to start preparations several days in advance and to cook for two or three days. These are joyful days well spent. And how better surely, to comfort, coddle or seduce than to put up a plate of crunchy fried fish, made golden with a virgin oil from the Molise area of Italy; richly studded with small slivers of garlic and fresh oregano leaves which have been lovingly cultivated in terracotta. What better than a fat chicken, stuffed with lemons, garlic and rosemary, served at room temperature, on pristine platters, laced with assorted green salad leaves and a scattering of fried sage leaves.

Healing powers

When I am overworked, anxious or stressed, food comforts and reassures me. And at every high point in life a celebratory meal, a feast, a zuppa di pesci, a fine ossobuco, or a mighty platter of meats and cheese, food marks the merrymaking and jubilation. Food can also bring me hope. It can restore me to positivity and optimism. The early days of the pandemic were days of empty city centre streets and blacked out shops; days when to walk in Edinburgh's main streets which had previously been thronging thoroughfares, felt frightening because I walked alone... the built environment succumbing to forces we could no longer keep at bay. In the days that followed, a friend brought me olive oil from the grove of a family friend in Picinisco. Still in the recycled Cinzano bottle into which it had been decanted, the oil shone wondrously golden, warm and strength-giving on my kitchen counter. To me it said: the earth goes on, the sun will return. You will embrace your people again.

Cucina povera... cucina di terra

The recipes in this book come from my experience of eating wonderful and plentiful home-cooked meals, and watching them being prepared, often in very basic kitchens, by women expert at their craft whose skills had been handed down through generations. These are women who know instinctively, by eye, by feel, smell or touch, how to get the best from whatever is ripe for the picking.

Homes such as these are where the culinary inventiveness and genius of Italy is to be found. It is in home kitchens where *la cucina povera*, *la cucina di terra*, a style of cooking that is basic, culled from peasant fare, based mainly on vegetables and pulses, often on leftovers too, is at its very best. This is *una cucina* which is unselfconscious, straightforward, coming directly from ground to table; it is fresh, nourishing, for both body and spirit. Meat and fish do show up; cured meats such as salami, prosciutto, cotechino and salsiccia too, but in small quantities, as trimmings, flavourings or for celebrations.

Rural Italy knows how best to respect the land and be alive to climate and the environment.

As Marcella Hazan, the goddess of Italian cooking, writes:

> There is no such thing as Italian haute cuisine, because there are no high roads or low roads in Italian cooking. All roads lead to the home, to *la cucina di casa* – the only one that deserves to be called Italian cooking.

My kitchen is basic with little equipment. I have an old-school Moka for my espresso and a cafetière for guests. (I leave the art of lattes and macchiatos to the many fine baristas around Edinburgh). My only real indulgence is a food processor. I smash garlic with a knife, separate eggs with my hands and beat them with a fork. I squeeze lemons through my fingers to catch the pips. And there is no better pesto than one you make in your kitchen in ten minutes. If you have nuts, a suitable herb (and most are), olive oil and garlic, you have a pesto! If you don't have a food processor, a basic grater or a mortar and pestle will do, though it will take a bit longer.

Lifestyle and philosophy

There is little more exciting for me than a market overflowing with aromas, purposeful people intent on getting the best cut for dinner, or a cheese that matches what is in the cellar; with newly pulled lettuces bristling with freshness, cauliflowers in magnificent bloom, onions ochred, yellow or pale and silky, garlic plump and purple (sometimes flamingo pink) trailing over benches, crowding and bulging from wicker baskets; and peppers, large and curvy, red as lanterns; all these make me giddy with excitement. And I see myself living another life in a small Roman kitchen, or a small French town, bustling about with gigantic stock pots, working dough and tending marjoram, oregano, mint and some rosemary perhaps, at my doorstep. Food is my constant life adventure. Between lovers and within family, it is interplay, bonding, enjoying the sweetness of familiarity brought by years. Food is flighty, often capricious on the stove and flirtatious on the chopping board, sometimes promising little and then to everyone's surprise, giving all and more, making you, the cook, proud. Food is also theatre, a song that reverberates around your walls, a beacon of hope and promise for a gathering, a common language with which we can connect. It is an aesthetic, and a wondrous example of the beauty within and around us in our world. Ultimately food can, across worlds, societies, cultures, seas and landscapes, link us directly to that elemental surge of life within underlands and overlands; and between all the layers of the wondrous planet we inhabit. Food is most surely the ultimate and supreme gift from this generous, boundless universe that we are privileged to share.

There is little science or chemistry in these pages. My inspiration has been those writers for whom recipes are not the whole story... whose interest lies equally in the culture, traditions and particular philosophy of life, purposefully articulated through what and who is in the kitchen and what food is on the plate. I can think of no better evocation of the shops and streets, the day-to-day of Rome's Testaccio district, than Rachel Roddy's stories about handfuls of herbs and her dealings with the local fishmonger. In *Tokyo Stories,* Tim Anderson brings the vibrant, bustling streets of Tokyo alive through his descriptions of fast food which provide a  fascinating and authentic insight into life in Japan. In *Ammu*, Asma Khan transports us right to the table of an Indian home kitchen. She weaves family history and memories with recipes and we suddenly find ourselves enjoying her mother's cooking with Asma herself, a child, among her many, excitable relatives. I treasure time spent with my cookery books (pictured above) as I do with dear friends and family.

Taking my lead from Nigel Slater and Jamie Oliver, as a general rule, I like to present my food on serving dishes in the middle of the table so people can help themselves. It is so appetising to see platters of heaped green vegetables drizzled with something tangy and glistening on one side, a deep pot of something sizzling and richly dark centre stage and a bowl of a herby dressing to be handed around. Helping yourself and others is also a lovely way of creating a sense of togetherness. For me, this is preferable to being given a set plate with all I might eat on it. It may be for that reason that almost as much as Italian food, I love the dishes of Spain, Greece, China, Vietnam and the Levant. Like an Italian table, every meal vibrant with colour and choice.

In this book, I have not been specific about measurements and quantities, or about how many people the recipes will serve. Experienced or inexperienced as you might be, I encourage you to trust your own instinct as a cook and adapt quantities and flavourings as you think appropriate but always keeping to the italianismo of it. Cheddar cheese is not an alternative to a gritty hunk of pecorino and bacon will never provide what prosciutto can give a dish (not even a prosciutto cotto will do). Quantities depend also on appetite and enjoyment. *Magnaccioni,* unashamedly may sometimes go well beyond what is commonly decent and why not? My own view is that it's best to make too much... leftovers, like a good Indian stew or a sugo from Venafro, generally taste even better the next day. Especially when they reappear as a pasta frittata, strands and moist egg temptingly entwined; or quite simply a pasta al forno, still rich and red, bubbling and bathed in mozzarella and pecorino.

Magnaccioni is then, less a cookery book, more a celebration of the people, culture, way of life and food of southern Italy. It is a book to be dipped into. The recipes I have chosen to include are all about flavouring and good quality fresh produce, requiring few ingredients.

Where I mention 'Italy' and 'Italians', generally I am referring to traditions in the cultural South... the Mezzogiorno... and very often, specifically to *la ciociarìa,* the culture, language and traditions in the area around Rome and Naples. Italy has only been a unified nation for 150 years. Its many dialects – 36 in all – each with its own distinctive sound, vocabulary and idioms, and its diverse traditions, still warmly resonate, especially throughout the South. Increasingly these 'old languages' are now celebrated in song and in the literature of today. Italy and italianismo, is then, a complex business. *Campanilismo* means one's cultural identity is defined by exactly where in Italy one comes from: *sono Toscano, sono da Milano, sono cresciuto in Sardegna* (I'm Tuscan; I come from Milan; I grew up in Sardinia). When I visit Milan or Florence, I am often asked where I come from or how is it that I speak Italian so well. In Rome and the south, that question is never asked. My Italian, south of Umbria, has come home. The further south I travel, the more fluent, or native, I become.

These regional, linguistic and cultural differences apply to food as well; to cooking styles, to choices about ingredients and to what people like to eat. That's what makes eating in Italy so exciting. The food of Rome is not the food of Milan. Nor is the food of Milan or Venice the food of Tuscany or Sicily. Somewhere in the centre of this colourful and idiosyncratic country, butter for sautéing and dressing a finished dish, becomes olive oil. Polenta and rice become pasta and patate... maybe at a pinch, crespelle (savoury pancakes usually stuffed and cooked in the oven). From Tuscany downwards, it is the glorious tomato in all its luscious incarnations, in all the different states of ripeness and colour that is queen of the kitchen in all that is required of it: be it a hearty ragú for pasta, a tasty topping for pizza, a rich sauce combined with grated pecorino for a bubbling crespelle or even as an alternative presentation of focaccia rather than rosemary and rock salt which is more traditional. Large, soft, misshapen tomatoes, vivid green, near black or a ruby red, or a mix of all three will add drama and sweetness to an insaladone (a big salad), and layered in large slices with stale bread and onions, kept at room temperature even for a day or two, will deliver mouth watering, irresistible panzanellas (bread salads). When stuffed with salty ham, gran padano cheese and breadcrumbs with maybe a chopped olive or two or a few capers, then toasted in olive oil in a hot oven, tomatoes can be stretched to a complete meal. For me, while I choose tomatoes in some form almost every day, I often have them for breakfast, grated or chopped on toasted bread, the tomato is particularly magnificent as First Lady in an insalata di pomodori con cipolla e olio vergine, (a tomato and onion salad with virgin olive oil). It is in the South that we also find lush olives and by extension, the prized first pressing of cloudy, green, smokey yet indulgently creamy oil from the hand-picked fruits of the grove. Exported italianismo... pizza and pasta, in no way come close to what Italy has to offer; it would be such a missed opportunity to think otherwise. Like its *lingua franca*, the common language, neither pizza nor pasta sumptuous as they are, fully represent the endless choices for meat-eaters, for lovers particularly of rabbit, boar, veal and even offal (a speciality particularly in Rome). On a peninsula where the sea is never far, the choice of fish and plump, fresh seafood is without limits as are ways of cooking them. And vegetarians can feast in equal measure on dishes of various lentils, on barley and on exciting dishes of tasty beans, be they green, fava, cannellini or borlotti.

The food of the South is unfussy. It reflects a people and a way of life that is mainly rural and which retains many of its traditions and in this part of the country, there is a strong culture of making the best use of what you have. Food revolves around availability and climate, what can be reused and the inventiveness and resourcefulness of home cooks. Never lacking is quality or integrity of basic ingredients or flavour. The food on the table is always fresh because it is linked to the land and to weather.

While the economy is lively and commerce is brisk in the vibrant North, in Milan for example, which in some parts seems to look increasingly to the US and the UK, as you travel deeper and deeper southwards life slows and one has the increasing sense of the prime importance of community and family. Serenely peaceful townships, turned in on themselves, appear scattered across the land, mountain slopes and valleys of the Appenine ridge and people seem to manage to live, often on very little. Yet, in my experience, in every home there is always a feast. Eating simply means eating well, there is no temptation to load or layer a pizza. No need to add more to a pasta, because with fresh ingredients, the best olive oil, the plumpest, fruitiest garlic, generously yielding tomatoes, and the lightest dough, no more is needed. What we have learned as cooks is to encourage the innate goodness of fresh produce to shine. We help broccoli to give its best greenness and iron packed goodness. We encourage peas to be as sweet as they can be and to bring out the contrasting taste of other ingredients. We enable smoky fish to boast its origins of salt and seawater. We look to the heart of the ingredients we have. Anna del Conte writes 'when you feel tempted to add more to a dish, add less'.

In the South, you will find the rich treasures of stuffed pasta, every vegetable elevated to stardom through the mere addition of a light sauce, a dressing or a way with locally grown herbs. There are so many cooking methods and inventive presentations for pork or fresh chickens. Every food is given its rightful place, dignified as a speciality. When the world praises the food of Italy for its distinctiveness, for its contribution to fine dining, for its health-giving properties, through, among other things, the use of flour, eggs, tomatoes and olive oil, it is the food from these southern parts, that has particularly charmed. It is unspoiled and it is always completely authentic.

Wine and music

For me a dinner without wine is unthinkable. While stories, recipes and words are what this book is about I have added suggestions about the wines I have enjoyed with the dishes. These are mainly wines from the regions of Campania, Basilicata, Lazio and further south. While what we choose to drink is of as much importance to an Italian as what is on the plate, equally, music lies at the heart of southern Italy. In the hardest of economic times, in the harshest of winter weather when villages are cut off for days, Italians will warm to a song that is full of memories or makes them laugh such as Massimo Ranieri's songs in Neapolitan dialect about the Italian suddenly turned American or Spanish; or the obsessive popper of pills. Humour is in the very soul of Italians and humour too in the words and gestures of language.

Very recently I was in Polignano a Mare, a beautiful resort of ancient bleached stone and terracotta saints and madonnas, by the sea in Puglia. Polignano is the birthplace of Domenico Modugno famous for *Volare,* the 1958 winner of the San Remo song festival. On a quiet Sunday afternoon, in the hot sun, suddenly, a male voice started up, singing that song. And whether seated at lunch, reading on balconies, drinking on terraces with friends, soon everyone within earshot (myself included) had joined in.

From the dances of courtship of a time that was, from the *ballarella* in small towns and village streets, to the opera houses of Palermo, Bari and Rome; from ancient choral music in the churches of Sardinia and Sicily, to the swing and sway of boats and romancing in Porta di Santa Lucia in today's Naples... music, like food, is a national religion and a way of life. To be startled by a sublime rendition of a Verdi aria (believe me, Italians know all the words!) or a song about love, the leaving of the land, food or mamma, from a building site, or a rooftop, as you walk down a street in Aquafondata or Cervaro, is not uncommon.

While what is on the table and on the stove sets the climate in my own home and a good slice of bread, maybe from Puglia, or the French baker nearby, lightly brushed with olive oil, make me more open and benevolent towards the world generally, a Vivaldi cello concerto or a Gaudioso mandolin piece, keeps me focused as I cook and Ranieri singing live in Naples as background makes my spirits soar, opens my heart and makes me dance.

And so, I offer you here, my own favourite musical accompaniments to cooking... playlists to opera, Neapolitan classics, new wave artists, singer-songwriters, traditional songs, baroque and classical music. I have wanted to evoke something special; that sensual, immersive experience that wine, good food and music bring us.

In offering all of this to you, I hope to bring the sheer joy and energy, the love of life that characterises Italians of the South, to your own table. I want to offer an inkling which I hope is infectious, as to what makes an Italian man rise in the stillness and soft light of morning time and in the warmth of a wakening sun, welcoming and promising, sit and savour the mists and the silence. I have wanted to share that delight in the world; to put into words as they unashamedly do, the attachment and connection to land, salt and sea that give life, that refresh, invigorate and make us happy to be alive on this, another day.

I invite you now, to start streaming the music, pour a glass of wine and cook for those you like and love.

Enjoy the book, the words, and the sunshine.

Buon appetito ragazzi!

A place to start

Music...

'Vitti 'na Crozza' by Antonino Castrignanò
from the album Aria Caddipulina

'La Societá Dei Magnaccioni' by Lando Fiorini
Souvenir da Roma, Cantaitalia

'Com'e faccette mammete' by Massimo Ranieri
'O surdato 'nnammurato (live)

LIGHTS, LAUGHTER AND an electromagnetic charge in the air that's hard to describe. Hard to put into words too, the sound of Roman, not Italian for that is another matter altogether, coming at us in continuous waves from every direction. The elegance of the city dwellers, who have exited flats and *palazzi* (traditional, historic buildings, their fine ancestral monuments, ornamented with pillared *cortili* (courtyards), grandiose *portoni* (heavy doors) and enormous *battiporte* (door knockers), for a night with friends, can be jaw dropping, dramatic, or just quietly cool. But it's the sweep and sway, the naturally confident, theatre-style air with which the something-year-old women approach a table which makes me stare; and the subdued, studied casualness of the menfolk which makes me smile in appreciation. This deeply rich language buzzing and humming around us in bursts and then torrents is like the food of this part of Italy... food that sings. Food that is so full of flavour that when you rise from a table, you smile both within and without.

I am here in Rome with my family. We are also visiting Viticuso, about 40 minutes by car from Cassino in the Val di Comino, a valley in the Abruzzi mountains through which flow the rivers Liri and Melfa. Viticuso is the village of my daughters' great grandparents on my mother's side. I am anxious to share this heritage with them and they feign interest remarkably well. At least I know for sure that they will enjoy the food that Aldo and Assunta will serve in their simple hotel L'Aquilone.

Assunta is much older than when we first met but despite her age, she is still known for her cooking. And passers-by who live in that small village continually pop in to chat, drawn in by the aroma from her kitchen. Or, having seen an unfamiliar car at the door, are curious to know what's for dinner. On a previous visit, some years ago, the sight of strips of dough, drying out on chair backs in their no-fuss, functional kitchen, compelled me to delay by some hours, my return to Ravello where I was staying.

Homemade tagliatelle, soothed in a bubbling pot to a gentle al dente and served for Sunday lunch more than justified that delay.

On this night, surrounded by my bright-eyed, intrigued girls, I am both emotional and proud at connecting them to their heritage. My voice drops a tone, my consonants and vowels elide and I am warm and settled in southern dialect mode. These are my people and I am connected in.

FRITTO MISTO WITH FISH AND VEGETABLES (FRITTO ROMANO)

The fashion for small plates hasn't bypassed Italy's south. On this our first night in Rome, my family and I choose an insalata mista (mixed salad) with a vegetable and fish selection cooked in a light, crisp batter, a fritto misto. My Coletta grandmother, even when she was financially comfortable after the harsh years of war, never wasted a thing. What arrived on platters at our table that night in Rome, decades later, was not too different from her gathering up of leftovers to make a delicious meal for the family all those years ago.

We ate prawns, monkfish, onions, cauliflower, artichokes, courgettes and broccoli in a batter, plumped and full-flavoured with tangy sweet provola cheese. On the side was a stylish gremolata adding a light herby delight and a small bowl of crema di peperoncini, a fiery pesto made up of chillis, garlic and olive oil, for loading and dipping.

In many Catholic families in continental Europe, whether practising or not, Christmas is celebrated after midnight Mass on Christmas Eve. The Eve is the main event for me and my family. These indulgent and elegant food delights are traditionally served then with a fizzing, chilled vino spumante to start, followed by an aromatic but gutsy white, both work wonderfully well. This dish also makes an indulgent, impressive starter...

THE BATTER

This quantity will cook enough fish and vegetables for 4 people. For more people, double the quantities and you will probably need to use two frying pans.

This batter stays crisp for hours and always works for me:

150g plain flour
2 tbsp extra virgin olive oil
200ml cold water
2 egg whites
a pinch of salt

Using an electric or hand whisk, beat the flour, olive oil and a pinch of salt into a smooth, thick cream. Add 200ml cold water until everything is blended and there are no lumps.

Allow the batter to rest in the fridge for at least 1 hour.

Just before frying, place the egg whites in a large clean bowl, whisk until they form stiff peaks, then fold them into the batter.

Heat the oven to 120°C.

THE FISH AND VEGETABLES

White fish, shelled prawns and pot-ready squid sliced into thin rings are all ideal for this dish. For the white fish, I generally use haddock, plaice or lemon sole but any fillet will do very well.

Cook the vegetables. I like cauliflower and broccoli best, broken into small florets, and courgette sliced into batons. But any vegetables of your choice will work... carrots, roasted aubergines, cooked sweet potatoes all work well.

Break the fish into strips about 3–4 cm in breadth. Dip the fish pieces, the prepared seafood and vegetables piece by piece into the batter and cook until crispy and golden all over. Have a heated ovenproof platter in the oven to put the cooked food on as you go, so that it stays warm and you can serve everything at once. Alternatively, serve as you go.

> With a fritto misto, some herbs and lemons are needed, their freshness will counterbalance the fattiness and density of the fried food. Lemons sharpen the taste experience and add colour. Fresh herbs will always enhance the flavour and appearance of anything you cook.

SAGE OIL

You may also want to add some sage oil. For this, grind torn sage leaves and a pinch of rock salt with a pestle and mortar until the leaves are broken down. Keep working as you add enough olive oil to make a wet dressing to be served with a spoon. If you don't have a pestle and mortar, use a blender.

FRYING

I find that a wide frying pan works just as well and is easier to use than a deep fat fryer. A point to note. I always use the best virgin olive oil that I can afford for almost all of my cooking, but vegetable oil is the best choice for this recipe because it has a much higher smoke point than olive oil... from 400–450°C.

Pour enough oil to reach 2–3 cm up the sides of a large frying pan, dip the food piece by piece into the batter and fry until your food bubbles and bristles with golden goodness.

For extra flavour and to complement the vegetables, you might want to add a thin strip of provola or fontina cheese or even parmesan shavings to the vegetable pieces before coating in batter.

And to Drink

My wine of choice for a fritto misto is a good Arneis from Piemonte. This rich and robust white wine replete with flavours and aromas of vanillin, almonds, peaches and flowers is a perfect match to the sumptuous array of mixed fish, vegetables, sliced lemons and crisp leaves on your table. Should you find it difficult to source, Viognier and Pinot Blanc are similar in weight and style.

antipasti...
relaxing with guests

Music...

'Terra Straniera' by Beniamino Gigli

'Passione' by Freddie de Tommaso
Decca, London Symphony Orchestra

AS ANNA DEL CONTE has said, 'An antipasto might consist of a few simple olives, or some slices of herbed cheese, or maybe just homemade bread, softened in the juices of tomatoes and olive oil.'

Un pasto in Italian, means a meal. *Antipasto* then, is what you eat before a meal. Traditionally, *il pranzo*, lunch and the main meal of the day, consists of an *antipasto*, a *primo piatto*... pasta, gnocchi or rice, followed by a *secondo piatto*, the meat or fish course. *La cena*, or dinner, particularly in the South of Italy, is eaten late, when the sun has cooled and is a lighter meal, maybe consisting of one course. During a recent visit to the south of Italy, I observed that the practice of a main meal at lunchtime, followed by an afternoon's rest, is still very common. While antipasti in Milan or Torino might be a dish of vegetables, soup... something to whet the appetite and add balance to a meal of fish and risotto, in Puglia and elsewhere in the South, antipasti are generally a much more lavish affair. If you are visiting the glorious land of *trulli*, those quaint squat houses with pointed roofs once used for storage or to provide refuge for labourers, in Alberobello for instance, your lunch, in the care of a fine home cook, may consist solely of several vegetables and pulses, followed by not one, but two pasta dishes. Or again, in Ostuni, the fine lady of the area, '*la città bianca*' or the white city, renowned for its palaeolithic remains and cathedral, your starters might be a light insalatina of seafood, with some broad beans lightly dressed in lemon juice and a bread so light and crisp it is, as the head waiter described it, '*criminale*'... I couldn't stop eating it.

My way of entertaining is to follow the traditions of the South. And I want to be with my guests, not closeted among my pots and pans while my friends and family chat amiably over their drinks. Since my dining and cooking area is small, I find it much more practical to have almost all my food prepared in advance. An ample, well-furnished antipasto can also be a relaxed meal in itself, a slow, convivial evening's event with drinks, or a lazy, meandering Saturday or Sunday lunch. And maybe to finish, a caffè corretto (perhaps with added sambuca or amaretto), or a small grappa or a Frangelico with a good espresso. You could always, too, eat the peach slices that have slowly been soaking in wine throughout the meal. I saw this iconic southern Italian tradition many times while staying in *laziali* homes years ago.

An antipasto of several dishes resonates with some of the finest culinary traditions in the world: the vibrant small plates of Spain; the vari-textured melt, crunch and creaminess of Middle Eastern food; and the deliciously aromatic steamed, fried or fresh dishes of Vietnam and Asia – fragrant spring rolls, rice cakes, finger-licking, sticky meats or ribs, vivid green kimchi pancakes, subtle lettuce wraps, sushi and bright, soft sashimi. Dishes of such variety and interest, artfully presented, on long, laden counters cannot fail to whet any appetite, however contained.

I cannot remember any meal in any Italian home, where there was no antipasto offered as a means of breaking a fast, or of picking at something tasty while enjoying the company and the wine. In the same way, six or seven smallish dishes to start a meal for four people, to return to again and again, often with a hunk of bread in hand, is to my mind not excessive.

This approach to leisurely grazing offers great scope for invention, artistry and creativity. I often lie in bed at night wondering what would look and taste best with a roasted cauliflower. Roasting generous slabs of cauliflower together with garlic not only smells but tastes delicious. Roasted heritage tomatoes look great. When I cook them fresh from a market anywhere in continental Europe, where baskets and boxes bulge with plump fruit, where every stage of ripeness has a use and gradually softens skins and honeys the flesh, where strings of cherry-red drape the counters, I need nothing other than some olive oil and maybe a little white wine with which to cook them.

Here at home in Scotland, by way of contrast, tomatoes are rarely sweet and succulent and creating flavour requires work.

For a tomato sauce, add balsamic for sweetness and acidity, a teaspoon of sugar or even honey. My Aunt Louisa put prunes in the simmering pot of tomato sauce, a family tradition she had picked up from her mother-in-law, Adelina Coletta. Adelina was private and mild-mannered, while Louisa, unpretentious and open, often sported a mink coat which she wore carelessly, like an anorak. Although so different in style, these two women co-existed amicably in the kitchen. Some families living far from home add oranges to their sugo, trying to recreate the fruitiness and balm of their sauces, roots and homeland.

A minced clove of garlic added to salted raw tomatoes makes them impossible to walk away from, as they quietly ooze their juices, into a virgin, fruit-speckled olive oil. They demand bread and it's wise to give in. Black olives offer salty spice and black garlic provides an element of fine dining, finesse and the promise of something yet more tasty to come.

Another preoccupation of mine might be how best to serve my roasted peppers. Scorched or skin on? With aubergines or without? Fried or roasted? I give careful thought to how best to lift the flavour of broccoli stems and what to dress my not quite hard eggs with. Anchovies or capers are often the answer. Maybe a little minced red onion?

An antipasto should be pure theatre, the spectacle of salumi (cured meats), leaves, vegetables and fish making your taste buds startle at the sight. An antipasto should have allure, too, causing a gasp as you present it and encouraging even the most polite of your guests to make a premature grab for their fork and succumb to the animal nestling within.

The following suggestions for antipasti are as diverse as the foods themselves, as are some of the methods of preparing them. That is the essence of an Italian banquet as I understand it. Some dishes can be put out in a few minutes, others will take longer. Some can serve as a meat or fish accompaniment, others as a meal in themselves. In some homes, a *nonna* (grandmother) or a *mamma* will continually rise from the table throughout the meal bringing out yet another dish, while the family show appreciation by hearty eating and happy laughter. I tend to do a bit of both.

Contenti tutti quanti! (Happy are we!)

FOCACCIA

The basis of any Italian first course, as you wait, as you sip and as you eagerly anticipate and wallow in the aromas, must surely be bread. Today, bread baskets have disappeared from most restaurant tables. Although in some élite eateries where portions are small, as much to be admired rather than eaten – art on a plate – designer chunks or seeded slices of various textures, flours and hues are presented as a rare delicacy.

My early life experiences of living in France and Italy as a student meant that any meal I put on the table was accompanied by a basket of the best bread I could source. Bread continues, for me, to be the stuff of basic, hearty eating. When you have eaten all the cannellini bean or tomato salad and some thick juices of oily, garlicky dressing remain, it is a matter of duty, surely, if not honour to mop them up with the softest of breads.

Focaccia is iconic, the queen of breads, to be eaten just on its own or as a supreme accompaniment to whatever else is on the table. In northern Italy, Liguria for example, it is often eaten for breakfast.

My home-kitchen focaccia is a precious gift from the first lockdown when I learned to bake it. It is a nod to my past and now accompanies many a meal. There is no better welcome surely than the smell of freshly cooked bread in any home. This recipe for focaccia works every time for me.

500g 00 flour
2 1/4 tsp dried yeast
2 tsp salt
3–4 tbsp olive oil
olives, thick-sliced garlic and rosemary or oregano
rough salt for scattering
350ml lukewarm water
(a little more if the dough is still dry)

Put the flour in a bowl and draw a line in the middle. Mix the salt into one side and the yeast into the other and then mix everything together.

Make a space in the centre of the mixture and pour in 3 or 4 tbsp of olive oil. Add the water very gradually, working the dough with a wooden spoon as you pour. The mixture should not feel wet but firm enough to be picked up as a piece.

Knead the dough on a floured surface for about 8 minutes. At the start, the dough will cling to your hands and feel a little tough. Keep kneading. You will know it's ready when the dough is smooth and your hands come away cleanly.

Place the dough in a clean bowl and cover with a dishcloth. Leave for no less than an hour in the warmest spot in your kitchen to rise and double in size.

Oil a shallow roasting tin if you want a traditional rectangular loaf. For a thicker, round loaf, I sometimes use a small cast iron frying pan.

Shape the dough to fit, keeping the same thickness all over. Cover and leave it again, for a minimum of 40 minutes. You can leave it for a bit longer if you want more of a rise.

Make thumbprints in the dough. Fill these with thick-sliced (not chopped) garlic and or green olives. Scatter over finely chopped rosemary or oregano and the rough salt.

For the salamoia (this is what gives the bread a glossy, golden appearance and creates a soft crust) pour over a mix of 2 tbsp of olive oil and 1 tbsp of warm water.

Cook in the oven for 20 minutes at 220/200°C. When the bread is darkly golden, remove from the oven. If you are in doubt about it being cooked through, switch off the heat and leave for a few minutes.

You can vary this basic recipe in many ways to suit mood and taste. Sometimes I add deseeded chunks of tomato, or a mix of tomato and black olives. Marcella Hazan adds cornmeal to her dough, finishing off her bread with delicious rounds of sliced lemons. Anna del Conte favours a classic focaccia Genovese style with nothing added except more olive oil before cooking. In Puglia, fresh cherry tomatoes, anchovies or cooked potatoes are added. Another version, popular around Naples, is to sprinkle fried sage leaves on the bread after baking and serve it with a tomato sugo or some warm passata, pizza style. This bread must be dipped! Source the finest olive oil and enjoy.

> Tip: Sage leaves are delicious deep fried. Dropped into hot oil, they change from moody green to silvery grey petals and will add a refined air to your fritto ensemble. You can also fry them in batter where they will take their legitimate place as a worthy vegetable in its own right alongside the finest of fish and its accompaniments.

PIADINE (ITALIAN FLATBREAD)

Piadine are wonderful on their own or as an accompaniment. They can be filled with sautéed greens, prosciutto or salami or a wedge of provolone or mozzarella.

The main issue here is whether or not to make them with animal fat. Most recipes include lard for an authentic piadina dough. However, I am not a lover of lard, and ever faithful to my roots, I use butter in my cooking very exceptionally... mainly to finish a risotto. For me olive oil is always best.

500g plain white flour
5 tbsp olive oil
5 tbsp whole milk
400ml lukewarm water
2 tsp salt
1/4 tsp bicarbonate of soda

In a bowl mix together flour, olive oil and milk.

Add salt and bicarbonate of soda.

Mix in the water, working the dough as you go.

Place on a clean work surface and knead for 8–10 minutes until the dough is smooth. Wrap in cling film for 1 hour.

To cook 8 flatbreads, divide the dough into 8 rounds.

Roll each flatbread out to fit a 20 cm cast iron or non-stick pan.

Place the pan on the cooker. When very hot, add each flatbread and cook for several minutes on each side, until dry, blistered and a little scorched in places.

Serve the stack at once.

Platefuls of Sunshine

I have a great love of Spain and an enormous appreciation of its cooking traditions. No country does garlic better or more fulsomely. Resorts apart, in Spain, in authentic eateries, food is just what it is. And my all-time favourite breakfast is pan con tomate, a simple dish of grated tomatoes served on bread with a side of olive oil and salt to taste. It is considered a staple of Catalan cooking, and Catalan identity too, but I have enjoyed it throughout Andalucia, in Madrid and Mallorca and as far north as Galicia. Italy has its own bruschetta (phonetically brusketta and not brushetta) of toasted bread, topped with olive oil and a pile of chopped, garlicked tomatoes, sweet cherry or any variety you fancy.

Tomatoes, chopped and marinaded in garlic, olive oil and a drop of sweet white balsamic vinegar, served at room temperature as part of an antipasto, will certainly, as it soaks and dispenses its favours of colour and taste, marry wonderfully well with focaccia and equally well with a rich Middle Eastern round loaf studded with halloumi or a salted, herbed feta. Tomatoes for a southern Italian are the stuff of their everyday... sheer luxury, mouthfuls of joy and a ray of sunshine on the plate.

The sheer variety of tomatoes in Italian markets is dizzying. Each has a different purpose. And sometimes the uglier and more misshapen they are, the more delicious they will taste when sliced or chopped... all the bounty of earth and sun gathered over the ripening process. I have learned that they are the most delicious and generous of all if they are a little overripe and thin skinned. For me they then give up their best.

As a general guide for these recipes, tomatoes whatever shape, colour or form you choose, must be sweet and at least soft.

Variety in colour – green, gold, yellow and deep, dark purple – will create a magnificent display.

MARINADED TOMATOES (POMODORI ALL'AGLIO)

This quantity will make a side dish for 2–3 people or a starter when combined with other dishes. If you want more, increase the amount of tomatoes and adjust the seasoning to taste.

*250–500g tomatoes on the vine, cherry tomatoes, grape
  tomatoes orange and yellow
extra virgin olive oil
salt
a splash of white balsamic vinegar
basil
1 clove of garlic (or more)*

Quarter your vine tomatoes, slicing horizontally first and then vertically. Half the cherry tomatoes by cutting horizontally. Half the grape tomatoes vertically. Add these to a wide deep bowl.

Finely chop and add the garlic.

Add olive oil, vinegar and salt to taste.

Leave covered at room temperature for at least an hour.

Add torn basil leaves then serve with wedges of focaccia, a piadina or a quality, bought, white sourdough.

TOMATO AND ONION SALAD (INSALATA DI POMODORI)

I first tasted a tomato and onion salad in Cordoba, that wonderful land of gitano subculture and flamenco, renowned for its historic 8th-century Mesquite with its astonishing blend of Byzantine, medieval and Renaissance architecture. It was here I saw beauty, grace and sexual power emerge from the ordinary and the unassuming: a woman in her 60s morphing through dance, into feral woman and reducing her three young male suitors onstage to a rhythmic crawl.

On a hot afternoon when the temperature rose to over 42°C, burdened with rucksacks creeping along stone walls to find shade in the city's Jewish quarter, we finally ducked below pavement level into what turned out to be a cool, city centre eatery, full of briefcases, polo shirts and shiny, well-tailored trousers. I remember the relief of stone cold white wine. It was an Albariño.

I still have a vivid memory of the magnificence of a tortilla, fat, rounded and deep, commanding, in the centre of a large oven; and the chef's full attention on it, to be certain it had reached the right consistency – tender, moist and crumbling yet firm enough to hold its shape when sliced, before, like Handel's Queen of Sheba, its grand arrival on the restaurant's counter.

What I have learned from that day and have incorporated into my own kitchen, is the joy of a richly flavoured, yet light, fragrant and fresh tomato salad.

Here is my version which I usually serve as part of an antipasto. It can be a side dish for a meal for four, a main accompaniment to roasted meats and salumi, or cured meats; to a delicate cauliflower and lemon risotto, or a more robust one, full and dark with mushrooms.

3 or 4 marmande, black heritage, red-ribbed, or any large, soft and yielding tomatoes
1 red onion, sliced very thinly in rings
extra virgin olive oil
salt
a splash of balsamic vinegar
1 tsp finely chopped fresh oregano

Choose a flat round plate. Cut each tomato horizontally into 4–5 thin slices and lay each slice individually on the plate. Place thinly sliced tomato on top. Create another layer in the same way. And another.

Add the olive oil and the balsamic vinegar and sprinkle with oregano or any herb... basil, marjoram, sage or even mint. Cover and leave for a good half hour.

STUFFED BEEF TOMATOES (POMODORI RIPIENI)

The genius of Italian cooking, is the ennobling of the ordinary vegetable. Anna del Conte's delicious zucchini al forno (courgettes with mint and garlic stuffing and her peppers ammolicati (peppers stuffed with breadcrumbs and parsley) are an inspiration; as are her aubergines stuffed with sausage, pine nuts and currants. Rachel Roddy's post lockdown recipe in *The Guardian* featured stuffed cabbage braised in white wine, her choice of a greyish white dish focused on taste rather than colour. And after months of the pandemic, during which the comforting indulgence of a blazing, self-satisfying red, red sauce dominated; oodles of sauce and more sauce for pasta, her recipe based quite simply on cabbage, was a cleansing, undemanding treat.

Ingredients for stuffing vegetables vary: from ordinary minced or sausage meat, to prosciutto cotto (cooked ham) ricotta, capers, currants and anchovies. From such choices at your disposal, any combination of these works. But there is a consistency in the abundant use of pecorino or parmesan cheese, breadcrumbs, copious amounts of olive oil and the use of beaten eggs to bind the ingredients.

Here is my recipe for stuffed tomatoes. They make an impressive addition to a buffet or a deliciously indulgent starter for 4–6 people. I like to present them nesting among wild rocket and a scattering of fresh, woody hazelnuts.

3 large beef tomatoes
55g diced pancetta
half an onion finely chopped
55g olives (green or black) chopped
115g pecorino or gran padano grated thickly
4 tbsp panko breadcrumbs
4 tbsp olive oil
1 beaten egg
oregano leaves

Oil a baking tray.

Cut the tomatoes in half horizontally.

Roughly scoop out the seeds, but not too thoroughly.

In a deep bowl, combine the pancetta, onion, olives, pecorino, 3 tbsp of olive oil and the egg into a stuffing.

Fill each half tomato with the stuffing. Top with the breadcrumbs and 1 tbsp of olive oil and oregano.

Place on the baking tray and cook in the oven at 200°C for 35–40 minutes or until the tomato bases are wrinkled, have virtually lost their shape and are cooked through. Serve at room temperature.

Mushrooms

The first time I made mushrooms stuffed with prosciutto, parmesan and pangrattato (breadcrumbs sautéed in olive oil) all bound with a beaten egg, followed by a full dinner of several courses, my guest apologised in advance for her behaviour and then lay down flat on my kitchen floor to recover herself.

Statistics show that the largest consumers of mushrooms worldwide are the Chinese but it seems that the Eastern world, and especially Latvians come very close. I quote from lifeinriga.com:

Latvians are bonkers about mushrooms… it's a national obsession. There is barely a single stretch of forest untouched by foragers come late summer and autumn.

The late Peter Mayle, author of *A Year in Provence* (1989) has been heavily criticised since his short-term spell of literary success, for having opened the way to an imperialist invasion of southern France by mainly English tourists. He does though, write well and with humour. I still have a charming mental image from reading his books, of queues of French people outside the local *pharmacie* after the first weekend of the mushroom season. Obedient and law-abiding, unlike their mercurial Italian neighbours, he describes Gallic hordes, standing one behind the other, in orderly fashion, their baskets full of mud and earth-bound cep goodness, awaiting the arrival of the local chemist to pick out any poisonous fungus that might be lurking in their booty from the wilds. For me, this cameo of life in provincial France pinpoints much that is French… order, containment and discipline. He portrays so well too, that delightful national preoccupation with minor matters of health and the *en masse* migration, emptying Paris, Montpellier or Nantes during summer months, to forest and wood; to *le camping,* or the *maison de campagne,* still a social marker and still in the family.

What Peter Mayle and others like him do, people who have spent long periods of time in countries which are not their place of birth, but who nonetheless endeavour to fit in and become 'native', is consciously emulate observed behaviours, silence the protesting self-observer and habits of a lifetime and fall in step with a wry, knowing smile. I can do the same.

When driving in Naples, for instance, when people blast their horns at a wavering truck, or wave their arms in the air while circumventing a car that does an unexpected emergency stop or delays to go forward on a green light, I too fall into that behaviour, finding the old gestures of my childhood home and those who frequented it.

In that part of Italy, I am able to freely rant about warm white wine, or the reheated brown mess of a sugo on my plate – behaviour I would not display in Torino, even less in Tuscany. I also cannot behave in these ways in Edinburgh for fear of being branded as uncouth or unwell.

In Paris, in one of the more renowned sweet shops in the city, awaiting the gourmet pleasure of a few deliciously, subtly crusted macarons with soft chewy centres I have decided to treat myself to… I temper my impatience and subdue myself to a meek expectant wait, while the two very lightly sugared, moist treats I have spent a mere four euros on as a luxury, a present to myself, are as carefully boxed and ribboned as if I had spent ten times more. That is the exquisiteness of Paris.

Like their Eastern European neighbours, Italians countrywide love their mushrooms, usually trifolati, fried in olive oil and garlic and finished with a squeeze of lemon juice or balsamic vinegar. Bruschetta with mushrooms cooked in this way and with the addition of oven-roasted cherry tomatoes is common, particularly in the autumn. Risotto with porcini mushrooms, cappellacci (pasta pillows stuffed with squash or other root vegetable) in a potato and mushroom sauce, or a glossy, porridge-like polenta, topped with sautéed mushrooms are all very popular.

I love cooking mushrooms. I enjoy the way they need to be gently coaxed into giving up their dark, woody, juices. And when I eat them, I enjoy the combination of moist firm flesh all the tastier with whatever has been added. Ordinary mushroom with gentle encouragement becomes a speciality food, valued for the earth that clings, requiring only the gentlest of polishing.

I have served the following dish many times. Friends have often asked for the recipe. Here it is.

MUSHROOMS WITH LEMONS AND WALNUTS (FUNGHI CON NOCI E LIMONE)

For a starter on its own with crusty bread for mopping or as part of an antipasto:

500g chestnut mushrooms
2 cloves of garlic
a handful of walnuts
extra virgin olive oil
balsamic vinegar
salt and black pepper to taste
a handful of chopped flat leaf parsley

Wipe the mushrooms with a damp cloth. Shorten and trim the stalks.

Slice the mushrooms vertically (2 or 3 slices, depending on size; take care not to make the slices too thin).

Place in a deep bowl.

Finely chop the garlic and add 2 tbsp of olive oil and the same amount of dark balsamic vinegar or lemon juice.

Add a pinch of salt and a good grind of pepper.

Mix thoroughly and leave covered with a clean dishcloth for 2–3 hours. During this time, turn the contents of the bowl over several times so that all the vegetables marinate. If the mushrooms look dry after an hour or so, add a little more olive oil and/or lemon juice.

Once the mushrooms look 'cooked', plump, soft and firm, adjust the seasoning and add the walnuts. Leave the nuts to soften slightly. Turn the contents of the bowl over once more. Transfer to a clean bowl.

Finish the dish with the parsley and serve.

Cauliflower

Another prime food is the full-blossoming cauliflower. Stately and characterful this previously unassuming but imposing vegetable, had been consigned to the ranks of an uneventful cauliflower cheese, or alternatively a soup laced with stilton (at best served with something crumbly and blue). However, for vegans and vegetarians to have something to munch on and ceremoniously carved, modern day cooking has enobled it; in the roasting, it equates to steak 'nirvana'.

Cauliflower speaks sulphur and things of the earth. When partnered with garlic, it sings more loudly, its earth voice more rounded and fulsome. Roasted or boiled as I hope you will find, cauliflower reaches the height of its powers with just a few simple additions as my own no-nonsense treatment of this noble brassica suggests.

CAULIFLOWER WITH OLIVES AND LEMONS (CAVOLFIORE CON OLIVE E LIMONE)

This dish works well as an addition to a combination of starters or as a side dish for meat or fish.

> *1 large or medium size cauliflower*
> *a handful of fresh pitted or marinaded black olives*
>   *(olives in jars or preserved in brine will not do)*
> *juice of half a lemon*
> *olive oil and salt to taste*

Break the cauliflower into small florets and boil until al dente.
Dress generously with olive oil and lemon juice to taste.
Add the black olives, salt and pepper, and combine.
everything.

The addition of chopped semi-dried tomatoes, their texture adding just a little more juiciness, also works well.

CAULIFLOWER WITH TUNA (CAVOLFIORE CON TONNO)

As an addition to a combination of starters or as a lunch for 2–3 people with good bread for cleaning your plate.

1 medium or large cauliflower
1 small tin of tuna chunks in oil
a clove of garlic
half a lemon
a handful of capers
a scattering of oregano leaves

Cook the cauliflower as above.

Mix with the drained tuna forked into small pieces.

Add minced garlic and capers.

Toss in a juice of olive oil and half a lemon.

Adjust the seasoning and serve.

Potato Salad

This potato salad is one of the dishes I remember my grandmother often making, as a fast food, if someone like the peckish parish priest happened to ring the doorbell late in the evening, or if we felt like something tasty after hours, more than her nightly routine of camomile tea. She would heat some olive oil in a frying pan, sauté an onion, sliced in rings until golden then add leftover cooked potato. She always used a wide pan so that the potato could cook and crust evenly.

Her combination of potatoes, scorched and crumbling, with

sticky, caramelised onions, rather like an Eton mess, was indescribably mouth-watering to behold, and pure gummy indulgence to eat. Years later, Franca a family friend from our Copper Kettle Café days now living in Brescia and the no-nonsense backbone of the household she shared with Rudi and their two children, reminded me of how potatoes treated in this way balance and enhance a cotoletta alla milanese (veal fried in breadcrumbs) or even a pollo milanese (chicken in breadcrumbs).

The following simple potato dish is also a winner each time I serve it. Cooked potatoes, lightly shaken to ragged in a colander, a little broken, so that when placed in a serving dish they pick up the flavours of garlic and of oil, well seasoned, are for me a pleasure that is almost elemental. The salad works particularly well with fish roasted or baked.

This is a chunky dish and the trick is to add all the flavours together with the olive oil when the potatoes are at their most receptive and warm, newly out of the pot. So drain, shake and flavour! Then leave the flavours to develop at room temperature and the potatoes to soften even more. Remember to be generous with your olive oil and adjust, along with seasoning, according to the quantity of potatoes and taste.

SIMPLE POTATO SALAD (INSALATA DI PATATE)

potatoes just cooked through but not soft
1 or 2 tbsp olive oil (more if you wish)
1 garlic clove finely chopped
fresh rosemary finely chopped
salt and pepper to taste

You might want to add deseeded slivers of tomato or a few sun dried tomatoes chopped in half; maybe a hint of fresh chilli, or some chopped green olives. Anchovies would work extremely well too, lifting and salting and adding another layer of intense flavour.

Smoked Haddock

Grandma lived in Viticuso until she was in her early 20s, and married there. She had never eaten fresh fish in Italy and I remember the careful reverence with which she unwrapped and ate baccalà sent by her cousins back in Italy. Baccalà is cured cod, preserved with salt. It needs to be soaked in water for two or three days before cooking. It is a speciality much revered by Italians countrywide, a celebratory fish, usually eaten in spring, during the Easter season of Lent and at festivals and major celebrations. In Naples and the south, it is claimed there are 365 ways to prepare it, a recipe for every day of the year. The recipes are as individual as the homes where the fish is eaten.

I can only imagine then, Grandma's excitement at coming to Scotland and for the first time, visiting a fishmonger or choosing from the display on the carts of fishwives passing through Edinburgh's Bonnington Road in Leith, a stone's throw away from the harbour; as they made their way into the city from Newhaven. She would have been, I'm sure, unable to believe her good fortune and her, now better, life.

Grandma loved whitebait which she made a point of ordering in advance from the fishmonger. She dipped the small fish in flour and fried them whole. On these days, the wider family would gather, the lights would blaze, the doorbell would ring with new arrivals; and there would be happy sounds of frying, laughter and the language I grew up with, from a steamy, crowded kitchen. She also particularly enjoyed smoked haddock. This she would lightly grill and eat (usually by the pair) with a fried egg on top, often for dinner, while I was happy with something a little less exotic. She would also turn to food when distressed or feeling unwell.

With her, from the age of about eight, I visited possibly one of the very few health shops in the city at that time. There she would buy herbal teas, olive oil and a supply of dried fruits and nuts, in particular figs which she loved, to tide her over until a fresh supply would arrive in a bulging cardboard box from Viticuso.

I, like her, love smoked haddock. And I have a warm memory of a hotel breakfast in Arisaig on the west coast of Scotland, where I was served an exquisitely shaped creamy-white fish, its edges turning near golden, flaky and soft, with a perfectly poached egg on top. The delicate flavour of the fish together with the thick, bright yolk, and buttered toast was a defining moment, one which I continue to recreate on my frequent trips North and to the Hebrides.

It will come as no surprise that I have included a fish dish in my antipasto suggestions and have named it pesce scozzese. Like the vegetables which need little to encourage them to sing and to stand out in their full glory, this fish only needs gentle poaching and the addition of some herbs, sage or oregano, a touch of good olive oil, lemon juice and maybe some garlic. But I think there is sufficient flavour in the fish itself without adding much more. You may prefer to grill the fish but for me, the poaching method keeps the fish at its most moist and tender.

The quantity given here is for a small addition to an antipasto, though I think the dish would be delicious served as an appetiser… the fish flaked on toast or on crostini (canapés which are bread based) with a slice of gherkin. To add a grassy freshness, you might consider slices of cucumber. All will combine nicely with a chilled glass of champagne.

SMOKED HADDOCK ITALIAN STYLE (PESCE SCOZZESE)

2 undyed smoked haddock
a quantity of finely chopped fresh parsley and dill
2 tsp olive oil
half a clove of garlic (if using) very finely chopped
juice of half a lemon

Gently poach the fish in water. Making sure that they are completely dry, put them on plate and flake them with a fork.

Add the olive oil, lemon juice and garlic, if using, and gently mix through the fish. If serving as an appetiser, make a small pile which you can spoon onto crostini or bruschetta.

Finally add the finely chopped herbs.

Artichokes

The artichoke is a widely revered vegetable. Aristocratic and distinguished, it has a kind of remote, aloof quality. On a trip to Rome years back, I tasted artichokes, neat and tight, each one green to purple, cooked in two ways: either alla romana or alla giudìa.

Cooked romana style, the vegetables, with outer leaves and choke removed and stem trimmed, are stuffed with mint and garlic and cooked in a delicate blend of olive oil and water. These woody, green/golden orbs of gentle luminescence, can be served moist with cooking liquid, into which you will want to dip as many slices of soft bread as you can. Alternatively, you may prefer them sliced and mixed together with all the juices through a pile of tonnarelli or even a short pasta like casarecce. In all cases they are exceptional.

Cooked alla giudìa, a fine example of Italian-Jewish cuisine, and a piece of the city's history, small artichokes are quite simply fried whole. Equally exquisite.

It feels as if artichokes have always been part of my life. I have so many memories of them, in France, Italy and in the on-trend restaurants of Edinburgh, Dublin and London too. I think of them abundant and full; a smokey green globe, neat and precise on my plate, or laden and layered with a melting, cheesy crust on and between every leaf. I think of white tablecloths, waiters twirling silver trays, green trees and long, lazy canals; bouncing boats tethered outside; swinging kitchen doors, the subdued expectant tones of French polite chatter, or again that reverent silence, when the food is good, when we are deep in concentration and all can be heard is knife and fork against plate.

I was in Milan some years ago, and on my last morning I returned to the cathedral area of the city. As I walked through the magnificent Galleria or the 'Salotto di Milano' (Milan's sitting room), as it is affectionately called because everyone meets there, the aura, splendour and chatter drew me to a small pizzeria. From there I had a view of the stunning Gothic spires of Milan Cathedral, a sight when you suddenly come upon it as you emerge from a busy street, that cannot fail to take your breath away. So startlingly bright and so architecturally uplifting as dentillation, spiked pinnacles and fine-crafted stonework take your eye upwards and beyond.

My white Piemontese wine was excellent. My artichoke pizza was sheer joy, the dough both soft and crusty. The corniccione (outer crust) was plump and round, charred black and invitingly crackled in places, by woodfire. Fine-cut fronds of artichoke, dribbles of olive oil and marjoram speckled and covered the entire pizza, complementing both the tang of woodsmoke and the understated refinement of the whole dish.

A good pizza is never loaded. Anna del Conte writes 'what you choose to leave out of a dish is as important as what you put in'. Describing the cooking of spaghetti alle vongole she dismisses the idea of adding more than one clove of garlic... 'leave the clams alone!' she exclaims. Pizza quattro stagioni or ai quattro formaggi, apart, a good pizza is, like all fine food for well-attuned palates, simple with one or two main ingredients. This pizza showcased only the artichoke: dough, paired with moist, almost transparent, leaves subtly and softly blended.

Malaga is a city I return to almost every year, usually just after Christmas for a rest after the cooking extravaganza of the festivities. Artichokes are never in short supply at that time in this vibrant city of food-loving, food-discerning people, but there is one restaurant in the city centre where artichokes are for me, the main attraction. On the first night of our first visit to Malaga amidst the bustle, hand-shaking and wide-armed hugging of the days before New Year, people re-uniting, families together at last, we fell into a wooded, cantina-like restaurant, with lively waiters all in black.

Amidst the happy brouhaha we ordered a dish of Serrano ham and artichokes. The ham was pink, thin and soft, beautifully kept and respectfully carved. But the main event for us was the artichokes. The entire dish was covered with succulent, tender hearts, glistening with the grainy olive oil that had nurtured them as they cooked, and lemon juice to taste. They were accompanied by an old-style basket of good, rough bread and extra olive oil on the side, should there not be enough. A fine bottle of Ribera del Duero, in my view Spain's best, stood by, awaiting our attention.

I first met an artichoke as a student in France, eating with wonderfully generous and hospitable families. Not only did we meet very successfully, the artichoke and I, but I also learned how to approach it with care and caution and I brought that new awareness home.

Over time, artichokes became a dish we ate as a family when we had guests. It was impressive certainly, but more importantly, any dish that requires you to use your fingers, bite, dip and even lick the leaves, is a great way for everyone to relax, barriers to be broken; to kick back and take time. For this is a dish that cannot be rushed.

One evening, a good friend came to dinner. We had decided that she was definitely someone suited to enjoying the experience of dealing with an artichoke as a first course. However, she just sat staring at the entire vegetable on her plate and the small dish of a dressing made of mustard, lemon juice, olive oil and honey beside her without doing a thing. After a minute, having looked around the table and in particular at my 4-year-old, Sophie-Louise, ripping, pulling, scraping and dipping with total ease, she got the idea and got to work. Artichokes are now a first choice on any menu for her and she still tells the story.

The basic way to prepare a globe artichoke is to clean it thoroughly and boil it whole for about 35 minutes or until the base of it is soft enough to put a skewer through. The leaves, as you pull them off one by one and dip into a prepared French dressing, become softer and more substantial as you approach the choke. Once you discard the hairy choke, all your endeavours are richly rewarded. The dimpled, grey-green, flower-like sphere appears, like a small grainy miracle, nectar indeed, made all the more flavoursome with a clinging, agrodolce (sweet/sour) dressing.

Stuffing or boiling apart, the way I like to eat artichokes best is *saltati* or sautéed. They can be served warm or left to cool and make a delicious starter on their own or added as part of an antipasto. On crostini they are elegant as a tasteful addition to the lively, salty flavours of prosciutto or an anchovy.

SAUTÉED ARTICHOKES WITH GARLIC AND LEMONS (CARCIOFI TRIFOLATI)

For 2 people you will need 6–8 large artichokes.

2 cloves of garlic finely sliced
1 lemon
2 tbsp olive oil
mint or parsley
a handful of fresh almonds, flaked and lightly roasted

Cook the artichokes as above in boiling water.
Discard the leaves and the choke.
Thickly slice the hearts.

Put the oil into a shallow frying pan which you will bring to the table. When hot, add the artichokes and the garlic.

When they begin to brown, turn them over so that they take up some of the oil.

Turn off the heat.

Squeeze the lemon juice over and scatter the herbs and nuts.

Bring the pan to the table and serve with a good bread or large slices of focaccia.

Broccoli and broccoletti

I like to steam or boil broccoli or broccoletti (longer stems and smaller florets) to just tender. I then sauté them in olive oil and garlic, often adding in other cooked greens, such as finely chopped cavolo nero, swiss chard, pak choi or even some lettuce hearts or peas. These are greens ripassati or twice cooked. I am not too surprised that children, especially in Britain, need to be encouraged to 'eat their greens', when they are merely boiled. But cooked this way, they are a joy.

In summer a simple insalata di broccoli is delicious: a warm salad with olive oil, a splash of good dark balsamic, some slivers of garlic and toasted almonds. Broccoli done either way works so well with a rib eye steak or a simple saltimbocca (escalopes of pork, chicken or veal cooked in white wine with parma ham added). It is equally tasty and adds substance should you be on a low carb diet, to any fish dish. With its yielding, tender stems, hint of sweetness, yet with a base line of minerals, you know it's good for you.

Broccoli can also take centre stage. This dish, added as an antipasto or served alone garnished with lemons will provide a mouthwatering starter. If the lemons are from Sicily or Ravello, all the better.

BROCCOLI FRITTERS (FRITTELLE DI BROCCOLI)

2 heads of broccoli
flour for coating
1 beaten egg
a quantity of breadcrumbs
(I find bought breadcrumbs unsatisfactory. You can easily make your own using a food processor or even grating crumbs of stale bread, and then lightly toasting them in the oven. If there is no time for this, panko breadcrumbs, lower in calories, sodium and fat and higher in fibre than other bought breadcrumbs, are the best substitute.)

Slice the broccoli keeping their tree-like shape and then blanch them in boiling water or lightly steam them.

Dip first in the flour, then the egg and finally the breadcrumbs.

Fry them gently in olive oil until they are crisp and golden.

Arrange them on a bed of crunchy lettuce and with quartered lemons.

You can make a fiery sauce for dipping by putting a few red chillis in a food processor, together with salt, a clove of garlic and add olive oil as you pulse to get the consistency you want.

Salumi (cured meats)

While vegetables and pulses are given serious attention in the South, and are an essential part of an antipasto, I feel I should say a little about cured meats. In rural Italy people traditionally still cure their meats at home: capocollo in Puglia; soppressata (pressed and salted meat) in Calabria; and prosciutto, salami and salsiccia, mild or peppery, (wrapped in handmade casings and hung for days) are to be found throughout the South. There is something heart-warming and nurturing about walking into a home kitchen and seeing meats hanging to air for sometimes 30 days. As a child, I heard many tales of piglets reared as family pets but ultimately taken to market.

Animal offal is widely eaten. Rome's Testaccio district is well-known for restaurants where almost every part of the animal is served as a delicacy, on its own or as part of a meat-based sugo. In Palermo's Ballarò Market you can feast on pigs intestines sizzling on the grill as street food, before picking up the fattest, juiciest arancini I have ever eaten, further along the street.

During a family holiday in Trastevere last year, led astray by my daughters after several 'dirty negroni' and in a mood of merry abandon, I ordered a pasta dish I didn't recognise in a very well-reviewed restaurant. It tasted delicious. Increasingly though, I became aware of the chewiness of the sauce. On closer inspection, I discovered small chunks of offal in the sugo. Undeterred, but being mostly vegetarian through choice, I continued eating, leaving the pale, chopped intestines piled at the side of the plate.

A simple affettati misti, a meat-based antipasto, adorned with a fruit, maybe firm sweet pears, or melon is delicious. Sometimes a well-deserved treat.

> Tip: For me, the presentation of food means half the battle is already won. So, when planning a meal, I give as much thought to how it will look as to what I will cook, and I choose my plates and platters carefully in order to show my food at its best. Over time, I have also learned about contrast and balance. For salads I choose a variety of salad leaves, colour and size which I pile and layer on a flat plate.

If you choose to offer a platter of meats as part of your antipasto, variety is key, and generous portions. What then follows can be straightforward, minimal and very simple; a stuffed chicken for instance with a sautéed green vegetable on the side; roasted leg or shoulder of lamb with mixed herbs from your garden pots.

And to Drink

Some of my choices for an elegant white wine to match would be a Vermentino Di Sardegna with aromas of oranges, lemons veering towards salt and to lime; or a Greco di Tufo from Campania, characterised by the tang of sulphur and clay soils with tastes of lemons, pears and roasted almonds.

An Aleatico from Lazio is a deliciously deep red wine, soft and dark with jammy fruit. Going more upmarket, a Cesanese del Piglio, medium bodied is worth the extra cost if you can source one. Going off message a big, powerful Amarone from the area just west of Verona, is easier to find and hard to beat.

Le frittate

brunch… lunch… easy dinner…
pre-dinner drinks… random snacking

Music…

'The Darktown Strutters Ball' by Lou Monte
Lou Monte American Italian Style: The Hits

'Parlami d'amore Mariú' by Mario Lanza
'Oi Mari' by Mario Lanza
Nessun Dorma… Greatest Hits, 2011

ALFIE'S PRIDE AND joy was his frittata and he delighted in his skill in cooking one. He was married to Louisa, my mother's elder sister. His parents, Adelina and Domenico had come to live in Blackpool from Pozzilli, a village in Isernia, not too far from Viticuso. My uncle Alfie often returned to Italy to visit a cousin who lived in Rome. Through these regular visits, he lost some of his rough edges while gradually integrating in grand style, into what must have been for Italian immigrants, the strangeness of Blackpool, with its side shows, night clubs, poker tables and black jack joints. His increasingly upmarket visits to Italy's capital, to San Remo and the French Mediterranean coast as he made his way into genteel society, made of him a well-tailored city gent with a penchant for fine dining. Smoked salmon, sweetbreads and the ubiquitous mink coat defined his and Louisa's outings to the best hotels on that Fylde coast.

My mother and I paid a surprise visit to them once in Blackpool. We drew up at their shop front, in my first car, a ramshackle, wobbling Citroën with its roof of canvas, of which I was very proud. Alfie, the proud owner of a sleek Daimler (its suspension always made me car sick), eyed our vehicle with both amusement and a twinkle in his eyes. Still wearing his Crosby style hat and a sleek suit as might befit a man of means from Rome's Via Veneto, grinning from behind the counter of their café on Blackpool beach, surrounded by Blackpool rock of various shapes (some dubious); monster ice cream cones and the place a-clatter with Lancashire voices and fake tan, he cooked and served us up the deepest, juiciest, most golden frittata I can remember. It was bulging with spicy, Italian sausage brought back from somewhere near Rome and a smoky cheese, maybe a scamorza; and made with a magnificent mix of 18 eggs.

My grandmother and grandfather grew up in the same village. They married on New Year's Day in 1910. Both were around the same age. They were young and hopeful; and my grandmother, coquettish until almost her last days, had no lack of male interest. She mentioned *gl'pisciadur* (chamber pot) several times when speaking of suitors on whose head she apparently emptied its contents. True or not, she kept men – son, grandsons, son-in-law, bank managers, doctors and business competitors, in their place and continued to do this until the end of her life, She also had a proud bearing and fine ankles which she showed off to advantage, sporting elegant, black court shoes until she could no longer walk.

As a couple, in Viticuso, Mariuccia and Emilio knew life could be better, easier, than the daily grind in a place so removed from the world and from opportunity. They envisaged an altogether different future. And so my grandfather and his brother serendipitously chose to venture to faraway Scotland, it is said, on the toss of a coin. Not long after, he sent for his wife and in 1913, Mariuccia travelled to Edinburgh to join him, with her small daughter in hand and another child on the way. The world was on the brink of the First World War; the Second World War to follow.

Before that move away from home however, together with family and friends, they worked in the home and in the fields, enjoyed tales, banter and song after dinner by a warm fire, went to Sunday Mass and made the very best of what nature, the land and the sunshine graced them with. Life, courtship and family were all straightforward; simple matters. Duty and responsibility were prime considerations.

Viticuso sits high above Cassino, beyond Montecassino Abbey. The road up is daunting and some parts feel precarious but worth the trip. Here, as in every village in and around, there is an abundance of good fare and stout-hearted women whose prime purpose is to feed their family as well as they can; even if all they can put on the plate is 'past' e patat' (pasta and potatoes).

While some of those who have left have over time, restored their family homes and return year after year, mainly for the feast of some saint or other, some of the old homesteads, those that survived the earthquake in the '50s, remain untouched, evoking history and old ways. It is hard walking the old streets, under archways, gazing far out over the fields not to imagine the daily terrifying thunder of shelling, which communities across the land endured daily for months during the Allied advance on Rome; the rampaging Moroccans and the bloody toll they took on mainly women and young girls and its fatal consequences; the arrival of Americans in village streets bearing candy for dark-eyed children all agog; the rubble and dirt that once was Cassino. And while others have lived through and watched recovery over the years, I always have both a deep sense of sadness mixed with an unsettling yearning for something I can't place after my visits. I leave both glad and reluctant too; and I visit to find what is no more, discovering instead, a land that the world has forgotten where men still play cards or take their leisure and women are ever unseen. Where unwilling young people who have moved to the cities to study or find jobs and a life, return for a while, showing off their newly acquired urban manners, style and sophistication. But I also have a picture in my mind of Emilio, a young, bright-eyed man of 23, in a bustling place early in the century, newly married, striding out to work in the valleys below the village, whistling that same old tune... valleys rich with the potatoes that my grandmother still spoke of until the day she died. He would have had with him a simple lunch of bread, onions, a mound of fresh cheese that my Grandma made so well, and a small flask of red wine in a makeshift bag of cotton, slung over his shoulder. His thoughts and aspirations went far beyond those mountains that contained them.

Like my uncle in Blackpool, Grandma too, made wonderful frittatas. I remember two particularly well. Her frying pan for both was equally large, having to accommodate no less than 12 eggs at a time and sometimes more. Each Easter Sunday morning, she would be up with the sun, singing quietly to herself, moving her rosary beads around. She had a bizarre ritual of making us suck a lemon on Easter morning, before eating or drinking anything. Then she served us a huge herb frittata which was quickly followed by a meat one filled with Italian sausage and some bacon. She didn't ever explain what these two frittatas symbolised but I did know that they bore some religious significance. Perhaps suffering and crucifixion, marked by the sourness of lemons. Herbs and eggs, symbols of healing, new life. Meat a sign of resurrection and celebration. The Christian story recounted in food.

Easter in the South, in Sardinia and Sicily is a mix of the profane and the sacred, much to the dismay still of the Catholic authorities who are, in some places, at pains to stop some of the more extreme, almost pagan practices, such as self-inflicted physical pain and suffering. One wonders whether, in place of belief and true faith, it is fear and superstition that have traditionally kept up the numbers attending Sunday Mass and observance of Holy Days in Italy. One such example is a recording made in 2013, of a lamentation, *u lamentu,* sung by male voices in a church in Sardinia. The very visceral wailing is intended to represent the grief of Mary at the first sight of her crucified son. And of all the various dramas of the Passion story, for Italians, North and South, it is Mary's suffering and the suffering of her son at seeing his mother's distress that is the dominant emotion, that brings tears; and is played out still, often by entire villages throughout Puglia, Calabria, the Abbruzzi and the South generally.

Catholic references and especially to the Blessed Virgin Mary, *la madonna* who has a special place in the heart of Italians, somehow always manage to find their way into streets, roadsides, cafés and corners, homes and discussions anywhere in the South and strangely, whether one is still practising or not. These can be prayers for help, for advice or an oath… *'mannaggia 'la maronna'* (damn… polite translation).

At its heart is the belief, deeply rooted from childhood and school, that the watchful eye of the madonna, when called upon, will always steer any enterprise to a good outcome. And, according to one remark posted by an unknown on the Giallozafferano website (a website 'to inspire Italian cooks') we find her in the kitchen during the whole process of cooking the frittata, standing by, should she be needed. As the saying goes: *Un uovo per ogni persona che mangerá la frittata, più un uovo per la padella, più un uovo per la madonna...* (one egg for each person eating the frittata, one for the pan, one for the Blessed Virgin...)

It is unclear how the frittata came about, whether from Northern Africa with whom it has a long history of trade or from Spain, a country with which it briefly shared a king. Even less clear is the genealogy of the French omelette. What is interesting is how this food has been adapted by related but very distinctive food cultures. The omelette française, often served in France for lunch, is made of two halves neatly folded over. Between each lies a melting layer of something soft, or creamy, or garlicky and redolent. The omelette features not the fillings which are folded in, but the eggs themselves, making them the star act. Its perfect incarnation is usually, unless you request otherwise, undercooked, like a good rib eye; and a little runny so that the tender, lava-like textures merge into a medley of mellow tastes.

The Spanish tortilla, on the other hand, is made up mostly of sliced fried potatoes layered and encased between an eggy base and an eggy topping. In order to feast on the luxurious contents with your eyes, before you taste you must cut deep, coaxing the luxurious ensemble to gently ooze on the plate at the first cut. The equivalent in Scotland could be a steak or Scotch pie. Like its Spanish older sister, an Italian frittata is made sometimes with potatoes but with the addition of other vegetables, or cheese or even cooked meats. The frittata is 'open-faced... fat and firm' according to Marcella Hazan in her *Essentials of Italian Cooking*. The frittata pleases the eye and promises a feast at first encounter.

It was in Chiavari in Liguria, not far from Genoa that I learned to make frittatas differently to the way I had previously seen it done, with fewer eggs. It was there I also learned to experiment with frittata ingredients that went beyond what I had learned as traditional. My tradition was to make frittata where the egg is thick and the filling usually provided a substantial flavouring. In Liguria I learned to reduce the number of eggs, to two or four so that they barely hold the ingredients together. To this I frequently add, grated courgette with parmesan cheese; mozzarella alone; cavolo nero with leeks and potato; sweet potato and feta; or quite simply, a soft ricotta which soothes my inner *anima* best.

Frittata however large or small is essentially a blend of complementary tastes, where strips of green might mix with potato, steam-softened, smashed, or even in crisped chunks, oiled and cooked first in the oven, piquant with salt and a flurry of mint. Or it might be made with sliced rounds of courgette, browned before the egg is added; or grated into slivers, which will sizzle in olive oil until well browned, and will only just be held together by the lightest, most delicate web of egg; then dotted, to finish, with a fresh ricotta or salted by a crumbled feta which has cooked to golden in a quick oven and is firm to the touch. But for total indulgence, there can be no more opulent frittata than a cheese one… a velvety, fondant blending of pecorino, scamorza, caciocavallo, and gran padano, enlivened, by small cuts of zesty prosciutto cotto bound in the depths of a soft, thick pillow of egg. A golden, gritty pangrattato will finish this dish with aplomb and crunch.

While there is a growing trend in *osterie* (informal eateries and different to a ristorante which is more traditional and more expensive) throughout Italy of offering frittatas as a light meal, generally frittata is seen a snack, the stuff of picnics or a cold lunch on the move. I have also seen it served as a tapa, a small *boccone* (or mouthful), a *stuzzichino* (a small snack) to accompany an Aperol spritz or a gin and tonic. In homes here in Britain with

Italian connections, frittata is well rooted and part of a tradition. It remains a healthy, nourishing meal. Whenever I have visited friends in the South too, a hearty chunk of frittata, stuffed with garlicky sausage, and freshly picked leaves of mint, may well appear on the table, to accompany a small glass of wine, or a limoncello.

Southern Italian food it seems to me, maybe more than anywhere else in Italy, makes a great deal of how to get the the best from leftovers and from what you have available. And frittatas, like the fritto romano, described earlier, are essentially about leftovers. It is worth noting here, that the food of the South has always, catered well for non-meat eaters. It is in the Mezzogiorno, because of the terrain, the remoteness, the adherence to tradition, the passing on from generation to generation of art and skilfulness, that we enjoy at their very best, local pulses: chickpeas and beans of every shape, lentils of all kinds. Here you will enjoy breads of many flours; and luxuriate in the rich, local endowment of vegetables of every colour, shape and size. It is in the Mezzogiorno, proud yet humble, that I believe we still see the true nature of Italian food. Produce which is local, is true to its native fields and terrain from whence it came, is largely untouched by other cultures. And a tradition which remains mainly unperturbed by change and the ever volatile tastes and fashions of the food industry and its consumers.

A successful frittata can be either started on the stove top and then finished in the oven; or alternatively, and this has always been my preferred approach, completely cooked on the stove top.

Once the beaten eggs have been added to the chosen filling, the frittata requires constant attention. Keep moving and lifting the edges, allowing the uncooked egg to be in contact with the base of the pan until all the egg mixture cooks.

At this point, in order to allow the uncooked side to firm up, either invert the frittata using a plate to allow the other side to cook, or place the pan in a hot oven and briefly cook at 200°C. You will know it is ready to eat when the top is nicely golden brown.

In the Buddhist Centre of Scotland's Holy Isle, where I was once cooking for over 40 guests, I used two catering sized pans and into each I put 22 eggs. Sensibly, since the pans were seriously heavy, we finished the frittatas in the oven. They emerged like heroines, bubbling and triumphant.

Whether southern style and substantial or the lighter northern version, a frittata is always about creativity, a sense of what tastes combine well and an eye always to how it looks.

For my frittatas I have two frying pans, one that measures 32 cm in diameter and the other 22 cm. For a substantial frittata, for 4–6 people, I use 10–12 eggs in the large frying pan. If I want a thick frittata for two, I use the smaller of the two for 4–6 eggs.

Frittatas have evolved over time… in a more prosperous world they can be sumptuous, made with the best of what can be found in food markets or grown at home; in poorer homes, such as that of my grandparents living in Viticuso, a simple frittata generally consisted of eggs from the family hens and onions which the land provided. It is that basic food that I want to celebrate.

> Tip: Adding a salty, smooth, grainy pecorino romano or a coarser, stronger tasting, grated parmesan would work well; even better with a little parsley or sage. And (even though I am not a fan of parsley), I suggest that this, Grandma's choice, will take your frittata to a different level.

A SIMPLE FRITTATA (FRITTATA DI TERRA) FOR TWO

6 eggs (or less, but no more than 6)
400g brown onions
olive oil
salt and pepper to taste

Slice the onion very finely.

In a bowl beat the eggs and add seasoning.

Cook the onions until soft in a generous serving of olive oil.

Add the beaten egg.

Cook until both sides are set.

If adding cheese, grate 150g of a hard Italian cheese and sprinkle over the top of the frittata.

Cook very briefly under a hot grill until the cheese starts to melt and bubble.

Alternatively you might add cooked potatoes roasted or boiled and then chopped before pouring in the egg mixture.

FRITTATA WITH SAVOY CABBAGE, ONION AND POTATO (LA FRITTATA CON VERZA, CIPOLLO E PATATE)

Serves 2–4 people:
1 onion chopped
half of one Savoy cabbage cored and sliced thinly and use the core too
3 small potatoes, peeled and thick-sliced
6–8 large eggs
olive oil
salt and pepper

Steam or boil the potatoes until soft enough to put a fork through. Blanch the cabbage.

In a large frying pan put a generous quantity of olive oil, enough to cover the bottom of the pan easily.

Cook the onions until they are starting to turn golden.

Add the potatoes and turn over the contents of the pan 2 or 3 times. It doesn't matter if the potatoes break up.

Add the cabbage and turn over again ensuring that all the vegetables have been in contact with the base of the frying pan.

Add salt and pepper to taste then settle the vegetables so that everything is equally dispersed. Now add the beaten egg.

Cook by constantly lifting the cooked edges and tilting the pan so that the uncooked egg fills the gap, and almost all the egg is no longer runny.

Then invert the frittata using a plate, and cook the other side for 2 or 3 minutes.

Let the frittata settle for at least 5 minutes and then slice and serve with a crisp salad. I use dolce verde or cos lettuce.

You can use this recipe for more people by simply increasing the quantity of eggs to 12, using a large cabbage and doubling the quantity of potatoes to 5 or 6. Once the egg is cooked on the underside, since the frittata may be too heavy to invert, cook the top by placing in a hot oven for about 10 minutes or until it looks cooked. Remove it from the oven, cover and let it rest so that it is thoroughly cooked through but still soft.

Frittata is also delicious when eaten cold. It makes a delicious lunch or snack. It can also be served in a panino or similar.

While other cabbages, green, sweetheart or even bok choy will certainly work for this frittata, for me and for the sake of authenticity, Savoy is my first choice.

FRITTATA WITH LEFTOVER PASTA (FRITTATA DI PASTA)

There are hidden, secret things that we do and never discuss or admit to; things that have no place in the public sphere. Often like Nigella in the early hours, we eat in secret, visit the fridge too many times, binge on a loaf of fresh bread, eat tablespoons of peanut butter straight from the jar, or like me, dine on a giant packet of olive oil crisps and several glasses of red wine. The popular *Guardian* podcast *Comfort Eating*, hosted by Grace Dent, is all about 'what do you eat when you're home alone?' Celebrity guests speak passionately about potato crisp sandwiches, baked beans out of a tin, pork pies eaten together with their preservative jelly, plummeting into an entire loaf of plain white bread loaded with butter. For me as a child, it was the jelly around spam in a tin that was my dirty secret. Clearly a rebellious act of anti-italianism… maybe a sort of steadying safety valve! Dent is a formidable food guru, but true to her roots, she is not averse to at times devouring together with her guest, their worst excesses, in her own words, like 'a wild animal'.

There is an iconic Italian eatery in Glasgow, Eusebi's Deli, which I visit whenever I am in the city. Recently my daughter and I ate a wonderful pizza there topped unusually, with mackerel and a white soft cheese. The award-winning owner, Giovanna, is a fine hostess and serious about her food. And 'Yesterday's Lasagne' is always on the menu. Amidst all the refinements of a well presented and carefully curated plate of pasta, leftover pasta, refried, is the open secret of many homes in Southern Italy. Everyone does it and everyone loves it; it is the dish we share with our children and intimates. Its equivalent is enjoyed in Central America, Mexico in particular, where refried beans, the pride of the Mexican kitchen, are a delicious staple and perfect when partnered with limes, huevos rancheros or a breakfast burrito. In Costa Rica too, they were served up to me at breakfast time along with fresh pineapple, mango and guava. I did eventually tire of it and of corn chips and salsa too which seemed to adorn every table in every eatery.

It was Rachel Roddy in *The Guardian* in 2020, writing about frittata, who exposed the practice of using leftover pasta this way. While Elena Ferrante gave me the courage to write about the rawness of life in Italy's south in *Language of My Choosing,* Roddy has legitimised my sharing of this recipe, inspiring me to share my delight at that glorious crackle, that satisfying stickiness of refried, scorched pasta which has gone from red to russet and the scent of which, of mellowed tomatoes, garlic and all the wondrous ingredients of sugo, the wine, the paprika or chilli, intensified, makes me wet-mouthed and giddy with anticipation. In my own home, leftover pappardelle or rigatoni, a favourite, coated in the tomato sauce that has had a first outing and then has been gathering strength overnight, is a dish that is frequently and seriously fought over. The flavour of refried pasta is best when the sauce is sparse and clinging, allowing the pasta itself to fry until crunchy. And a pasta frittata cooked in the oven, topped with grated parmesan cheese or on the stove is even better. Add just enough egg to showcase the pasta and its crust. The more visible the pasta the better.

For 2–3 people:
a quantity of any leftover pasta in a ragù
olive oil as required
6–8 eggs

Beat the eggs in a bowl.

Heat the olive oil in a pan large enough to ensure that all or most of the pasta has contact with the heat.

Fry the pasta until it crusts a little, then add the beaten eggs and cook evenly as before.

MOZZA FRITTATA (FRITTATA CON MOZZARELLA)

Around the corner from where I lived as a child in Edinburgh's Bruntsfield – now a hip district with wine bars, hotels abundant with florals decorating the door, windows and surrounds, industrial chic places to hang and drink coffee, eat over-full bagels, revel in shakshuka, patatas bravas and hummus of all kinds and colours, or nibble at a humble scone bulging with cheese and jalapeño – was the iconic health shop where Grandma bought her herbal teas and nuts.

She had a friend, a traditional Scottish lady, who had managed Shrubhill Café, the family restaurant in Leith during the war years, and who still visited from time to time. She always wore a hat which she kept on her head throughout the entire evening and was a strict vegetarian which was rare in those days. (I guess vegetarians didn't do so well for food choices in the '50s and '60s.) Speaking of which, in Kirkwall in Orkney in the '80s, I was offered cheddar cheese and chips for a veggie dinner while my family dined well on burgers.

Grandma's friend was so thin that she once bent over the arm of a wooden chair and broke a rib. Whenever she was due to visit us, Grandma would set sail early, elegantly clad, not forgetting her chic hat and white gloves, to her health shop, in order to provide appropriately for her friend (clearly, Italian food would not do). The health shop was where she also bought rennet, which she used to separate fresh milk into solid curds and liquid whey, in order to make ricotta which only she ate. So strong was her belief in all things fresh and natural, she dismissed the ubiquitous yellow and orange cheddar cheeses of Scotland and worse still, the rubber slices of processed cheese which was all the rage in the '50s and '60s. I have a cousin, Gloria, who still makes ricotta in the old way.

Grandma had a small, battered pot kept only for cheese making and I have a memory still, of a small, slightly pockmarked white cheese curd, proud and set, in a tiny sieve, sitting on our gas stove awaiting Grandma's knife and fork. It would be eaten later and if muzzarè (in Neapolitan dialect), or mozzarella, was popular in Naples and the South, we Italians in middle class Edinburgh knew nothing of it.

Muzzarè, the defining cheese of Naples, used for pizza, frittata, and as a topping for many oven baked dishes, was made originally from the rare milk of buffalos. It is maybe best known for its stunning role in melanzane alla parmigiana (aubergine parmigiana) a sumptuous, layered dish of aubergines, mozzarella and parmesan softened in an abundance of olive oil, then baked in a hot oven, into a melting fusion of texture and taste set against the golden tangy skin of roasted parmesan cheese on top.

Italians as we know, cook according to what is seasonal. When aubergines are no longer available, often courgettes are used instead. And in the autumn, that mellow season, sumptuously golden pumpkins or squash are used instead. However, the original aubergine version, which first appeared, not surprisingly in Campania and in Sicily (its close neighbour), is famous and eaten across the world.

My first visit to Sardinia, where we stayed in a beautiful rented villa just outside Alghero and sat on the veranda listening to the sea every night singing random songs, was a journey of discovery... of unspoilt beaches, of the perfect art of melanzane alla parmigiana and a quest for what wine would be best with it. I returned home understandably, buttons popping, several kilos heavier.

Naples mozza is also the basis of burrata, cheese paradise, even for unbelievers. Burrata is a refinement; a development, a succulent and subtle combination, a tempting fat pouch, of mozzarella, which forms its skin, and when cut open, collapses to reveal an indulgently liquid filling of curds and cream which demand no less than a speckled fruity olive oil and over-ripe tomatoes, as partners; and all piled on to a chunk of good bread. You may even be tempted to add more than a trickle of a good homemade pesto.

A mozza frittata is an omelette for two or three people rather than a frittata. It is a dripping melt, enfolded and oozing from within a lightly fried casing of cooked eggs.

4 eggs
250g mozzarella sliced thinly
olive oil
a handful of toasted flaked almonds

Beat the eggs and then cook them on both sides in a frying pan.

Add the cheese and almonds to the middle of the omelette.

Fold both sides of the omelette over the filling and make sure that the cheese is covered.

Cover the whole omelette with a lid and turn off the heat.

After 2–3 minutes, the cheese should be melting.

Remove from the pan, slice and serve.

THE EASTER FRITTATA (FRITTATA PASQUALINA)

For a family with healthy appetites and enough to return to later.

18 eggs
150g Sicilian, Calabrian sausage or cured Italian sausage from an Italian food outlet
150g diced smoked pancetta
150g cubed provola cheese, caciocavallo or grated parmesan

Prick the sausages and place them in a pan of boiling water to get rid of the fat. After a few minutes, remove them from the pan and slice them.

Cook them with the pancetta in a hot frying pan.

Beat all the eggs adding salt and pepper.

Add the cheese to the egg mixture.

Add enough olive oil to coat the bottom of the pan.

Add the egg and cheese mixture to the meats in the pan.

On a medium flame, keep lifting and moving the egg around until as much egg as possible is set.

At this stage you can either continue to cook on the stove or put the frittata in the oven.

If you continue to cook on the stove top, invert the pan and cook the other side.

Then invert the pan again, cover completely and extinguish the flame on the cooker.

You can check whether the frittata is thoroughly cooked by inserting a fork in the middle of the mixture.

When well cooked through turn the frittata out and serve in wedges or cut across it to create rectangles.

And to Drink

Corvo Bianco, Duca Di Salaparuta from Sicily is a lively straw yellow wine that is worth seeking out. It is crisp, light and with a satisfyingly rounded flavour.

Should you prefer a red, Corvo Rosso, is like a Nero d'Avola in style, ruby-red, full-bodied with aromas of dark morello cherries, and stands up well to the richness of this dish. An excellent choice and a wine that I have enjoyed for many years.

Music

'E Lucevan le Stelle' by Enrico Caruso, from Puccini's Tosca, Act 3
The Complete Victor Recordings, 1990

'Mandolin Concerto in G major: Allegro'
composed by Domenico Gaudioso, version by Artemandoline
from the album Concerti Napoletani per Mandolini, 2018

L'ORA DELL'APERITIVO... RITUAL AND MIXOLOGY:

SWIFTS AT DUSK, massing overhead... high above old city walls and spires; over basilicas, temples, arches, palazzi, the ancient, rococo and baroque of Rome, of Naples, Bari, Lecce and deep into the South; this is not the solid and dignified Renaissance of Florence or Siena. Giddy, they wheel and circle, adding voice to the animation and energy of facial expression, gesture and speech, edgy, unpredictable traffic and exchange in the bars and cafés, and to the gutteral language of the southern lands. The birds and their freedom, their triumphant, feeding cantatas spicing your negroni, your Campari soda on ice and oranges, Martini or Aperol spritz.

This is an experience I will not forget. This the Italy I seek when I am far away. This is the encounter I look forward to when I return to my hotel room intent on a cold shower after a day roaming the teeming, over-full streets. The day's heat has cooled, the stones, marble and mosaics of the city are still warm to the touch, night and the sun's afterglow fills the sky. *Motocicletti* zipping by, car horns honking, police cars hoot-tooting, and the glorious mayhem and pulse of a city or town. People who love to live; who love to talk; who love to watch and listen. A curious people, inquisitive and interested in the character and lives of others, Southern Italians are often wise, philosophical, resigned to the downturns and childishly gleeful at the best that life offers. And I sit back, inhale it all. My appetite for dinner, the night and tomorrow growing by the minute, I relax and consider my choices and I contemplate this Italy that is like nowhere else; this Italy and people that can often frustrate me to madness, this Italy that I know and love so well.

When I was a student in Florence with a small part-time job to pay the rent, I often passed Cantina Frescobaldi, a wood-panelled, dark enclave of discreet elegance and exquisite finery and tradition. Frescobaldi is one of Italy's oldest wine dynasties with several wine estates throughout Tuscany. I returned to the street years later, more able now to enjoy its offerings. I went in, rubbing shoulders with, who knows, possibly, members of some of the oldest, historic aristocracies of the city: Strozzi, Medici, Tornabuoni, Pazzi, perhaps. In the company of Marchesi, Visconti and Duchesse, there I enjoyed the finest crostini, topped with the chicken liver paté that Frescobaldi is famous for... pungent with added capers, garlic and parsley, and all finely balanced by a full-bodied, robust Chianti.

It was further north, in Mantova, Ferrara, Milan and Venice that in recent years I became aware of the sanctity and ritual around *l'ora dell'aperitivo* and with all that partners a glass of something vaguely bitter, an appetite stimulant (in the unlikely event of it being necessary), at the end of a busy day. As a descendant of immigrant people from a tiny hilltop hamlet, where living and survival were rough, this langourous, more comfortable, chic Italy where people took time, enjoyed their leisure, and dinner to come is slowly anticipated, was a sudden and happy revelation. I experienced this particularly in Mantova, that less-visited Italian city of lakes, of Renaissance and medieval structures; of Monteverdi and music; and the birthplace of Virgil. There, in the stately, remotely situated church of San Francesco, we hovered to hear a Mass sung, full-throatedly by a black congregation. And in Mantova we discovered a hidden gastronomic treasure. Leaving our rented cottage, a traditional structure made of old stone, of ironmongery, architectural styling and exposed brick within; and our well-hidden city centre courtyard, where the low sun fell on olive trees, and sandy ground, we emerged, seeking a good dinner and followed our guiding star. We slid, one behind the other, through the heavy-framed timbered door and turned into a busy street. We saw ahead of us an avenue of bars, people of all ages thronging around doors and counters, chatting at overcrowded tables. We passed, entire buffets of pizzette, meatballs, frittate, small quiches, crisps and olives. It was *l'ora dell'aperitivo,* the magic hour, and we could sample all of this for the price of a Garganega or a vino rosato.

In Ferrara days later, we ate delicate tramezzini, tiny sandwiches layered with ham, soft cheese, a random tomato, and lush pizzette dressed with the scantest of toppings; in Chiavari near Genoa we had farinate, small chickpea pancakes. In Milan, during Fashion Week (a week of icons, high prices and *alta moda* (haute couture), we ate savoury pastries of prosciutto and pecorino with a bubbling wine from the Franciacorta area.

On another occasion, in Venice, during the sometimes outrageous Biennale art fest, we were treated to neat spinach arancini soft, half split and crumbling in a rich warm sugo; un' tramesin (Venetian dialect) literally stuffed to bursting with a mix of mortadella, prosciutto and provolone cheese, and cut into tiny triangles. With them, a prosecco superiore from the prestigious Valdobbiadene area. In Torino, in Piazza Carlo Felice after an extravagant shopping expedition, we ate an entire tray of savoury puff and choux pastry, small quiches and small rectangles of focaccia topped with creamy flakes of cheese, slivers of tomato, mounds of fresh ricotta and caramelised onion accompanied by one of the best Aperol spritz I have ever tasted, more alcohol than ice.

South, in Sardinia, our drinks came with pan casarau (Sardinian dialect) music bread, olives, and elegant, salted, fresh almonds from nearby orchards; and in Cassino, small hunks of salty parmesan brushed with olive oil accompanied bruschette with pecorino and garlicky mushrooms; and tiny pizzas topped with a homey ragù.

On café terraces, on corners, on chairs that swing and swaddle, on church steps and even astride the low wall of an iconic fountain, throughout the entire country, after hours spent selling high fashion and the day-to-day; sitting at a computer screen, or behind the counter of a bank or in a newsroom of *La Stampa* or *Corriere della Sera*, people congregate. From the offices of Oggi, a long-established weekly mag, after penning pieces of gossip about icons of fashion, the music world and the British Royal Family, sharing snippets that we in the UK never see, they meet.

Before going home to dinner, friends come together; and students gather to chat about a class in philosophy or literature, or maybe even to eat for 'free' as much food as they can manage. If at 5 o'clock in Paris, as rumour has it, 'all the city is making love', in Italy, the entire country is taking the air, taking a breath, inhaling the sea air, letting the sounds of their town or city wash over them and enjoying warm fellowship. Whether in slick, sophisticated Milan, Umbria, that land of ancients and saints (St Francis was born here), Florence or Lucca or Siena with its reputation for parsimony, or Bari where they hug, smile and cry all at the same time at seeing you, Italians find joy in human nature and in their neighbours.

And if you are fortunate, as you enjoy these many treats, of taste, sound and surroundings that hum with heart, you may even come across group from *i Musici di Roma* or *i Solisti Veneti,* rehearsing a little something, somewhere in a cloister... a Capriccio maybe by the less-known baroque composer, Locatelli, or a Corelli sonata.

Crostini are said to have evolved from the Middle Ages when Italian peasants had little food to eat and were forced to survive on whatever scraps they could find, using stale bread as plates. The bread often had to be softened with wine, olive oil or whatever was to hand. Bruschette are usually made with a rough, sourdough (or similar) bread. Crostini are much smaller, usually round and thinly sliced, allowing the temptations that top them to sing. For that reason, bruschetta is often served as an antipasto, whereas crostini, a mere mouthful, are widespread at parties, formal functions and big events. They come usually on crowded platters served by black-clad waiters who also pop bottles and serve you with fizz. Or again, they are to be seen furnishing contemporary side tables, in grey, industrial design houses, on boards, or on spare, Swedish-style crockery.

At Christmas last year, while my family roamed the kitchen quietly, impatiently, scavenging and trying not to hurry the Christmas Eve feast I was preparing, I threw a few crostini together gathering what I could find in my daughter's fridge. I cut bread into small, almost bite-sized pieces, brushed them with olive oil and placed them on an oiled baking tray in a hot oven.

I turned them over once and when toasted, I topped them with roasted tomatoes and garlic which oozed satisfyingly into the crusts; mozzarella cheese which softened with the heat from the bread; San Daniele, paper-thin and meltingly soft and placed a charred sliver of asparagùs on top. They looked elegant and went well with our Christmas drinks… a sparkling prosecco and a Negroamaro wine, from Lazio, red and full-bodied with lots of spice.

> Tip: Here is a list of possible toppings:
>
> charred artichokes and gorgonzola;
>
> smoked pancetta with roasted cherry tomatoes;
>
> cooked, minced Italian sausage with capers;
>
> black olives, anchovies and capers blended and served on green leaves;
>
> melted brie or soft cheese with caramelised red or brown onion;
>
> ricotta, radicchio and sautéed mushrooms;
>
> to finish… a sliver of lemon, truffle oil, chilli oil, garlic infused olive oil.

TRADITIONAL CROSTINI (CROSTINI SEMPLICI)

Makes 12 small crostini:
500g chicken livers
1 onion
a splash of white wine
2–3 anchovies
1 tsp capers
olive oil
1 cup chicken or vegetable stock

Fry the onion and then add the chicken livers. When cooked add the wine and turn up the heat to let the alcohol evaporate.

Put the cooked mixture into a blender and add the anchovies, capers, a little stock and olive oil. Keep adding until the mixture resembles a tapenade.

Add salt and pepper to taste and serve on crostini while still warm.

And to Drink

In London's Southwark area, a hip, happening place selling sophisticated vermouths of every hue and provenenace is the place for people to be seen and where you can choose your dry or sweet vermouth, from a head-spinning list of possibilities. The bar/eatery is somewhere to linger and 'a veritable playground for your palate'. Sicily, Calabria, Naples and around all produce some excellent vermouths. For me, a negroni cocktail (made with Campari, gin and a sweet vermouth) or an Aperol spritz aside, my choice is a vino abboccato which is slightly sweet. Sardinia produces some excellent ones, Cacc'e Mmitte from Lucera for instance. Or, an Orvieto Classico Abboccato from Tuscany is an elegant choice.

The best of life

Music

'Tammurriata Nera' by Nuova Compagnia di Canto Poplare
Musica Napoletana, 2020

'A Finestra' by Carmen Consoli
Eco di Sirene, 2018

'Io vi amo... Deliro, ti amo... Sono pazzo'
from Cyrano de Bergerac, opera by Franco Alfano,
sung by William Johns and Olivia Stapp,
RAI Orchestra and Chorus, 2004

STROZZAPRETI AL POMODORO in Acqua Al Due in Florence, a place of aged wood and spotlighting, vaulted recesses, memorabilia and proud tradition; and fresh pasta, the prize, among many other dishes. This is not Rome, far less Naples, it is contemporary and yet typical of the style, mood and presentations of much in this legendary city. Here walked Savonarola, the fanatical monk; the infamous Borgias; the glorious Lorenzo dei Medici and the creators and craftsmen of cathedrals, paintings and sculptures that launched us as a civilisation into a new era of the arts, science and philosophy. The conversation here is a low, continuous soundtrack. My youngest girl, age four, at the promise of pasta, is looking around her, big eyes and wide smiles. She can already taste it. So can I.

Strozzapreti pasta are a novelty and I choose them because the idea of 'choking priests' oddly appeals. And they do resemble a rope, these small textured twists, the contours, creases and cavities catching a delicate simple sauce of fresh tomatoes, some barely broken, a dribble of the finest Tuscan olive oil, more green than golden, and about which we are now expert since we are staying on a working oil and wine estate, *le Ginestruzze* near Montespertoli and about 15 miles from Florence, The parmigiano is optional. The food needs no chewing, soft mouthfuls of deliciousness, pasta, sauce and cheese are one.

Pasta is eaten throughout Italy but in the South, unlike elsewhere, it is a daily occurrence, and along with bread, it is a staple, whereas, in the north of Italy, in the river Po region of Torino, Cremona, Piacenza and Ferrara, rice and polenta are more common. Risotto alla milanese is an iconic, saffron scented dish from Milan to which butter and parmesan are added. Risotto alla milanese is either eaten on its own as a *primo piatto*, or as an accompaniment for ossobuco alla milanese, a dish of succulent veal shanks, enriched with bone marrow and cooked slowly in white wine, lemons and parsley.

Risottos feature in the south too, not creamy or cheesy as in more northern areas, but infused with white wine, stock and at times tomatoes. In Salerno a risotto might showcase fish and seafood, beans or lentils; or again, vegetables, such as peas, fennel, artichokes, courgettes, porcini mushrooms or simply, sweet, fragrant lemons.

What makes the difference between a paella, a pilaf or Chineses fried rice, ultimately (apart from the rice itself), is the essential, signature addition of the *mantecato*. It is that final flourish of added butter and parmesan cheese which elevates the dish to the elegant, epicurean speciality that it is. Without a mantecato and an arborio or carnaroli rice, what lies in front of you is not a risotto.

Polenta too, more typical of the North of Italy, deeply rooted in Piemonte, Veneto and Lombardia, takes a different twist in the South. The same is true of crespelle (pancakes), a dish widely available throughout Veneto, Lombardia and Liguria. In southern regions crespelle are paired with what is grown locally, topped with a tangy southern cheese and bathed in sugo; a true feast for the eyes and the food of angels. Because of these traditional and cultural adaptations, people in the North are sometimes 'affectionately' labelled *polentoni* (polenta eaters) and in the south, *mangiamaccheroni* or pasta eaters! These descriptions seem to sum up the differences rather well.

If there is one pasta that conjures up Rome, both its antiquity and its workaday, it must surely be fettucine, wider and thicker than tagliatelle, an altogether more rounded, more satisfying plateful. They are easy on the eye because they are an elegant pasta... a few prawns, a fleshy lobster tail, or white crab meat strands, whatever is your preference, nestling within lightweight, ribbony folds. Alternatvely, they may be simply served, moistened with butter, a little mascarpone or freshly made ricotta with nutmeg and parmesan scattered on top. Or again, the strands, full and soft, might arrive at your table, flush with artichoke leaves, fragrant with olive oil and small mounds of ricotta, crumbling as they are served. Paccheri, oversized, rectangular, hollow parcels, also very common, are often matched with hunks of roughly minced of beef or lamb; and with rabbit, wild boar, 'nduja (a spicy, spreadable pork sausage) or cotechino (a large pork sausage which is slow cooked). Tonnarelli, a larger type of spaghetti, are usually cooked all'amatriciana (with bacon and a tomato sauce), or in a blend of caciocavallo cheese and pepper – a cacio e pepe sauce.

These pastas moulded to their purpose of meat, earthy vegetables and strong, rough cheese, are an eloquent articulation of the South's heart and very soul. They stand for history, tradition and custom. They speak the language of generations, in humble dwellings, in times of drought, earthquakes, storms or floods when crops failed and there was little from the land. They speak of hardship in times of war, times of political unrest, times when recovery was slow and food choices very few. Pasta and bread, potatoes and cheese have been a means of survival. The food we see on menus now in Rome, Bari, Naples and elsewhere are a fine testament to the women who created them to feed large families and a tribute to the farmers and farm workers, bakers, gardeners... hardy labourers compelled through economic necessity to seek work far from home.

While men used whatever they knew best and could do in order to provide, it was traditionally women's work to feed and clothe. Lace-making is one of the lost arts of Viticuso and the villages around Frosinone and la ciociaría but I am still awestruck today to meet the many women in villages near to Viticuso who treasure that legacy of skilful use of needle, thread and cloth; of weaving and making. These precious home-based skills of dress making, tailoring, altering and even designing clothes have served generations of immigrant families very well as they made their way as strangers into a new way of life with at the start, little to support them.

Grace, fine cloths, candelabra and tradition reside still in Villa

Maria, one of the finest restaurants, owned by the Palumbo family, in distinguished Ravello, a township high in the Appenine mountains overlooking what many say is the most glorious coastline in the world. From such a vantage point, as you sip your house vermouth with a slice of Sicilian orange, you will be enthralled at the spectacle of white stone, terracotta and marble… villas, fountains, and twisting streets of Amalfi below.

Positano too is nearby, only a short boat trip away. Here, yachts and boats and tackle, bump, bob and nudge, singing their own sea shanties to the sky. You can speculate as you gaze, about how to live a life; or about the 72 flavours of gelato artigiano (homemade ice cream) which are within reach by car. And while deciding on what you might eat here in this refined food palazzo, the view, the menu and the aromas of fruits, vegetables, select meats, fresh and lush, will all conspire to weaken your will, encouraging you to let it all go.

It is with great pride that Villa Maria, cooks and serves the food of the South and spoons into your plate, if you are fortunate and they are on the menu, crespelle as fine spun, as artful and light as new lace. Sadly, on my first visit, I didn't order crespelle, but I tasted my partner's and was smitten. The pancakes both enfolded and were caught in a light sauce of tomatoes and grated cheese and I cannot remember anything so delicious, nor so soft in my mouth. There is a mistaken belief that a *primo piatto*, be it crespelle, risotto, polenta or pasta, is heavy. Over time, I have learned that done well, by a discerning chef with a light touch, all of these dishes are as airy and tender as butter or a Japanese noodle.

While this part of Italy is jaw-droppingly beautiful, there is a distinctly otherworldliness about the villages of Puglia where sounds, smell and light, are unlike anywhere else I have been in Italy. This is life lived on a different timescale with a beat and rhythm of its own. In the beautifully, untouched, post war, Pugliese town of Cisternino, in the South, where you can buy a glass of wine, sit in the square among baroque and medieval buildings, churches, ancient dwellings, their stairways worn down with the passing feet of ages, and nibble freshly barbecued chunks of meat brought to you by the butcher himself.

The light is going down as we contemplate dinner. The glow catches the stonework, the old metal doorhandles, the paintwork shrivelled and dried by the sun, when from nowhere, we hear the sound of an accordion. I look up a side street and am warmed, and emotional at the sight of a couple, hard to say their age, maybe in their 70s, dancing a slow, graceful waltz. They see only each other, both maybe reliving something of a romance of another time.

In Locorotondo, Lecce and throughout Puglia, land of bright blue sun-studded seas, of excellent wines that can compete anywhere in the world we find the small gems of orecchiette pasta. It is a legendary pasta possibly originating from Norman times or Jewish culture, and only made by hand with wheat from the Tavoliere delle Puglia, a plain in the northern area of the region.

All over this land, eateries still exist in some corner where the dining area is makeshift, the converted public room of a small house, the cook in her own kitchen right behind you – and small dishes flow. The orecchiette, those tiny, ribbed cups or 'ears' are served, brimming with a clinging tomato sauce that has reached its best, at a long slow simmer on the stove, vaguely fiery with added chilli; and a plateful that you scoop up in shoals with a large spoon. Or may come served green-flecked, tossed in olive oil, fried garlic and broken spears of broccolini (longer stalked baby broccoli) or cime di rapa (turnip greens) and finished with a generous helping of pecorino romano. In many restaurants you may not even see a menu. And it is even more unusual to see a wine list and indeed it would be impolite to even ask for one.

For every area, a pasta that is native and for every sauce, its own pasta. For every Italian home too, a family favourite. We like our pappardelle or paccheri dripping sauce from within and without, quickly drained; some retained pasta water added to a sauce of fresh tomatoes, cooked down to almost a stew, making it even richer. We like our sauce when the colour has turned and when it coats the back of a spoon. We like our paccheri glistening, slick with olive oil, but first rinsed pink with sugo in the pot, then turned out, topped with sauce, then mascarpone which slithers slowly along every strand, combines with the sauces, and maybe a few roasted cherry tomatoes, or black olives and torn basil scattered throughout. Pecorino is passed around the table as is a dish with extra sugo.

As to my visitor who ate my carefully considered and highly regarded pappardelle, with her knife and fork, left much of it uneaten, and concluded her somewhat impolite behaviour by announcing that she didn't like 'big pasta' – well she was never invited back. Clearly, we had nothing in common. When my daughters come home though, I don't need to ask what they want me to cook. I grew up with pasta every Sunday and a ragù based on hough or shin of beef, both cuts ideal for slow cooking and Grandma pot roasted the meat whole. A ragù, (from the French word *ragoût*) possibly introduced during Habsburg rule in parts of Italy and throughout Europe from the 15th century until the late 18th century, is a meat sauce or sugo for pasta. Some of the best recipes for ragù are to be found in Hildebrand and Kenedy's *The Geometry of Pasta*. Marcella Hazan provides an excellent recipe for a ragù di agnello, a lamb sauce, from the Abruzzi region. Rachel Roddy, writing about the food of Rome, offers a mouthwatering recipe for potato gnocchi with a pork rib ragù.

Some notes on preparing pasta

Caz Hildebrand and Jacob Kenedy hit the nail on the head in *The Geometry of Pasta* when they say:

> Centuries of Italian invention, industry, agriculture, hunger and politics have shaped pasta into its myriad of forms and flavours. Few (if any) of the shapes described were designed by any one hand... Instead, subtle differences have increased as methods to prepare modern Italy's staple food have passed from mother to daughter, neighbour to neighbour and town to town. The startling diversity we wonder at in the natural world is mirrored in microcosm in pasta. Evolution is at work.

Here are a few suggestions which will ensure you enjoy your pasta experience to the fullest.

Every length and shape of pasta has a purpose, an ideal mate, its own perfect partner for gourmet perfection. The list of long and short ribbons, of pillows, of studs, buttons and strands is long. Some pastas are destined for soup and healing broths. Some add balance, and are made to carry big flavours and are an ideal foil for chunky or spicy meats. Some by their very design will naturally blend with and showcase the finest seafoods from the sea around and beyond Italy. Others small, fine and gentle, will act as an undemanding, aromatic prelude to your meal, matched very simply with a few herbs, or a clove of garlic, or 2 or 3 anchovies.

Paired with the right sauce, and because of its subtleties and finesse and the care that goes into its making and shaping, pasta is a simple dish worthy of gourmets. It is to be savoured and enjoyed of course but most importantly, it is a dish to be given the full honour of a fine dining kitchen.

It is vital that pasta has plenty of room to be free and to float in the pot. I have a large stock pot which I use only for cooking pasta. A pasta pot is worth the investment.

The pot should be 7/8 full and when the water has reached a rolling boil, add the pasta.

After adding the pasta, move it about once or twice so that it doesn't stick together or to the bottom of the pot.

After 5–6 minutes, keep tasting. Personally, despite the experts, I like my pasta cooked through, not al dente but also not overcooked. This is a matter of choice.

When the pasta has reached its optimum 'cookedness', remembering that it will continue to cook for a minute or so when removed from the heat, add 2 ladlefuls of the pasta water to your sauce which will be quietly simmering, ready to be served. Drain the pasta and return it to the pot.

Run a small amount of olive oil through the pasta, stirring it well and then mix in some of your sauce ensuring that all the pasta is coloured.

As you peer into the rusty richness, bubbling on the stove, casting spells of spice and tomato around your kitchen and among your guests, who will be by now babbling with childish anticipation, reaching for bread, gnawing a breadstick, munching a stray olive or two, and certainly salivating as you work, you will be able to exercise your special rights as the cook: surreptitiously sweeping up the salty clinging crust of tomato around the rim of the saucepan. The crusty outer ring of a pizza, the corniccione, is in some pizzerias, treated as separate from the pizza itself. Often, in London and elsewhere, a pesto, a gremolata or a pepperoncino dip is offered to compliment it. The same distinction could apply to the gritty sauce left behind on the rim of the sauce pot while the sauce cooks down. A few chunks of very good bread can turn this leftover into a cheeky antipasto for the cook only.

To serve, put the pasta on a large platter. Top it with more of the sauce keeping some back to be handed around. You may want to place a tablespoon of mascarpone on the top, or add some toasted pine nuts; maybe a few black olives halved. If using pecorino, pass a bowl of grated cheese around the table. You may even wish to roast a few cherry tomatoes and scatter them, charred and cracked, along with some basil or fresh oregano.

Pasta merits the status of a plate rather than a cereal bowl. Pasta is best enjoyed when eaten with a fork and spoon. Italians do not use a knife and fork because the sheer pleasure of the food lies in the rolled mounds, or even spoonfuls if using short pasta, of pasta and sauce which you gather on your fork and with the help of a spoon if required, pop into your mouth.

Here are some of the sauces that I enjoy cooking. I hope they give as much pleasure as they have in my home.

A BASIC BEEF SUGO
(RAGÙ NAPOLETANO/RAGÙ DI MANZO)

Slow-cooked meat in the recipe below takes this sugo to a different level. This is a dish for my family, of epic distinction. It is festive, unctuous, irresistible, impossible to stay away from as the sauce develops slowly, darkening in the pot and casting its tasty aromas into the sweet repository of treasures and good things that is your kitchen. I have never been able to resist dipping as it cooks, my lump of bread dissolving in meaty, tomatoey goodness. A challenge to my aspiration to be a total vegetarian, a happy capitulation and a glorious fall from grace… my taste buds more than satisfied with what is in my mouth, mellow and moist. The meat takes on the oily richness of the sauce it has cooked in; reciprocally, the meat releases its strength and vigour into the thickening liquid in which it is gently maturing. You will need:

3kg hough or shin beef in a piece
4 cloves garlic crushed and chopped

2 tins peeled tomatoes
2 tbsp tomato purée
1 or 2 tsp sugar to taste
olive oil

Brown the meat on all sides in a sauté pan.

In a separate large pot with a lid, heat enough olive oil to cover the base of the pot and cook the garlic until just beginning to take on colour, then add the tomato purée and cook for a few minutes.

Add the browned meat and the peeled tomatoes. Wash out the tins with hot water and add to the pot. Then add boiling water until 2/3 of the meat is covered. Stir the liquids well.

Season well and add the sugar to taste.

Bring everything to the boil, turn the heat down to a simmer and cover the pot. The sauce should be neither sweet nor bitter, the flavour deep and rounded.

Keep checking the tomato mixture for taste and consistency. It should resemble a sauce but it should not be thin; the richer the better.

After about 2 hours, remove the meat from the pot and store in a warm place.

When the sauce is rich and flavoursome, add it to cooked and drained paccheri, rigatoni or a chunky pasta of your choice.

Serve the pasta then carve the meat into good-sized slices and serve separately.

In many homes in the South and in my own, the meat is eaten after the pasta often with a salad or some cooked greens, lightly tossed in olive oil and garlic. Another variation is to serve the meat, carved into chunks, with the sugo and mix everything through the pasta. This makes a very substantial but delicious dinner.

RAGÙ DI SALSICCIA

This sauce was a great favourite at Easter and Christmas in our house.

1 onion finely chopped
1 leek finely chopped
1 stick celery finely chopped
2 carrots finely chopped
2–4 minced cloves of garlic
3 italian sausages from an Italian food outlet
1 tbsp tomato purée
2 cans peeled tomatoes
1 cup red wine
salt and pepper
1 tbsp fennel seeds

Remove the skin and roughly chop the sausages.

In a large wide pan, sauté the onion, followed by the celery, carrots garlic and leek.

When all the vegetables are soft add the sausages and cook until they have taken on colour.

Add the tomato purée and the fennel seeds.

Add the wine and let it boil vigorously for a few minutes.

Add the peeled tomatoes. Fill one of the cans with hot water and add to the pan.

Bring everything to the boil and then reduce the heat to a simmer.

Add seasoning and cook for about half an hour or until the sauce has thickened and everything is cooked through.

A LIGHT TOMATO SAUCE (SUGO DI POMODORI FRESCHI)

There are times when all you want is a light pasta dish as either an undemanding meal, a meal when you have nothing else in the house, or a delicious starter, with more to follow; maybe roasted rabbit or chicken; one of Hazan's lamb stews; or hake, coated in breadcrumbs, garlic and parsley and lightly fried.

This sauce will do for 350g of pasta. It is a fresh, almost fruity sauce if cooked without any spice. When I cook it, and it is so easy and quick to make, my aim is to break down the small tomatoes while retaining some of their shape and natural flavour. The garlic and seasoning are added to encourage the natural flavour of the tomatoes to emerge. If you add any chilli, or ginger, or fennel seeds, or whatever takes your fancy, you are adding another layer of flavour and complexity. These variations also have a place.

250g cherry tomatoes halved
1 cup white wine
2 cloves thinly sliced garlic
salt and pepper to taste
1 pinch chilli powder (optional)
8 basil leaves, shredded
olive oil

In a medium-sized pot, heat enough oil to just cover the base of the pan.

Add the garlic and after a few seconds add the tomatoes.

Cook for a few minutes until they break up and then add the white wine. Turn up the heat and let the wine sizzle for a few seconds.

Turn down the heat to a simmer.

Add the seasoning.

Cook for another few minutes until you have a sauce of tomatoes which still have shape then serve.

Add the basil to garnish the pasta.

Orecchiette (small ears, like cups), casarecce (short twists of pasta from Sicily), cavatappi (hollow corkscrews), strozzapreti (small twists of pasta, rolled into tubes, like a noose), capelli or capellini d'angeli (thin strands or angel hair), cavatelli (elongated, small and tube like and popular in Molise, Val di Comino and Calabria), short rigatoni (ridged tubes) are all ideal for this light sauce. It is also a good pairing and quick sauce for ravioli and gnocchi, and can be added to a risotto or used as an accompaniment to polenta cooked as a porridge.

A MEDIUM TO RICH TOMATO SAUCE (SUGO DI POMODORI)

This sauce is the one I cook most regularly, and I usually cook it in a large quantity and freeze some. My general approach to cooking is to over cater and I am liberal with sauces and with the flavours I add. There is never too much olive oil or garlic. Food from southern Italy is not for the faint-hearted. Nor does it need anything else except cheese in slivers, sliced with a vegetable peeler or roughly grated.

You can choose whether or not to make a soffritto (a vegetable-based stock). It certainly adds flavour and is very much worth the trouble.

Pair this sauce with a chunky pasta. The more sauce through and heaped on top, the better. And just to be sure, more sauce handed around is a safe approach.

First a note on skinning tomatoes: Place all the tomatoes in a large pot. Pour over enough boiling water to cover them and bring back to the boil. As soon as the water boils, turn off the heat and let the tomatoes cool. As they do so, the skin will crumple and crack. Drain the tomatoes and the skin will come away very easily. Chop ready to add to the sauce.

THE SOFFRITTO (OPTIONAL)

1 onion finely chopped
1 leek finely chopped
1 stick celery finely chopped
2 carrots finely chopped
4 cloves of garlic minced

Put in enough olive oil to cover the base of a large pot.

Sauté all the vegetables and garlic and cook them very slowly until they have released all their flavour.

Purée them together with the tomato paste, and put the mixture back in the pot. Add a little more olive oil and add the skinned chopped tomatoes.

THE SAUCE

This is a sauce for 1–1.5kg of pasta (enough to feed 6 healthy appetites with some left over).
20 large tomatoes (choose overripe and soft skinned)
6 cloves garlic, crushed and finely chopped
2 tins chopped tomatoes
1 tbsp sun dried tomato paste
2 tsp sugar
1 tsp smoked paprika (hot or sweet)
olive oil
1 cup red or white wine

Cook the garlic until just turning colour, add the tomato paste, cook for a minute and then add the skinned, chopped tomatoes.

Soffritto or not, proceed as follows:

Add the contents of 2 tins of chopped tomatoes to the pot.

Pour in the red or white wine and let it bubble for a minute or two. Fill the empty tins with boiled water and add the water to the pot.

Give everything a good stir.

Add another cup or two of boiling water.

Add the paprika, the sugar and the seasoning.

Stir again and bring everything to the boil.

Lower the heat to a simmer and cook slowly with the pot half covered until the mixture has turned colour and reduced to a sauce that will coat the back of a spoon.

Keep tasting the sauce as it thickens adding seasoning and spices to suit your palate. This should take around 40 minutes.

If you want a thicker sauce, continue cooking for a little longer.

Fettucine or tagliatelle (flat, long strands), pappardelle (large, very broad strands), and paccheri (short, rectangular tubes) are my favourites for this big pasta dish. Maccheroni and ziti, which are long pasta tubes, and campanelle, which are bell-shaped tubes, will also hold the sauce well.

This sauce was also my grandma's base coating for pizza; rather than a traditional focaccia al bianco, she dribbled a tomato sugo over a focaccia which was crunchy, golden and garlicky on top and light and crumbly beneath – the result was no less than food paradise.

TROFIE WITH PESTO (TROFIE AL PESTO GENOVESE)

My version of pesto is light, using only herbs, nuts and olive oil. While adding around 50g of gran padano or pecorino, or both, is included in some classic recipes, I add these later to the finished dish.

You can vary the looseness of the sauce according to taste. It should just hold its shape, be glossy and even slightly grainy. This is such a simple sauce to make. It takes around five minutes and tastes so much more vibrant without all the additives in shop bought varieties. (This quantity will make an average sized jar of pesto which can be stored in an airtight container in the fridge.)

For the pesto (pesto di basilico):

200g basil or about 6 shop bought packets
200g virgin olive oil
100g pine nuts or almonds toasted
salt and pepper to taste
2 good-sized cloves of garlic

Put the basil, leaves and stalks, 80g of the pine nuts, and garlic in a food processor and spin.

Reserve a handful of the nuts for scattering over the finished dish. After a minute, start adding the olive oil. Keep checking the consistency until you have a sauce.

When you are happy, season well and put a tablespoonful on some soft bread, pour a glass of white wine, a chardonnay grape variety which will stand up to the earthy, garlicky sauce and enjoy the first 'pressing'!

TO MAKE TROFIE WITH PESTO:

3–4 tbsp pesto
500g pasta

Trofie from Liguria are traditional for this dish but equally, casareccie, strozzapreti or any small cut pasta will work well. I sometimes even use linguine.

> Into a large pot of boiling water, add 500g of pasta, enough for 3–4 people.
>
> When the pasta is cooked according to taste, drain it but keep 1 or 2 ladlefuls of the pasta water to mix with the pesto and through the pasta, until pasta, water and pesto combine and the whole dish is a light, spring-like green.
>
> Scatter over the remaining toasted pine nuts or almonds and a few torn basil leaves and serve.

TROFIE WITH POTATOES AND GREEN BEANS
(TROFIE AL PESTO, CON PATATE E FAGIOLINI)

Although many of my visits to Italy have been to the South and to Florence, I have recently spent some time in Liguria, Lombardy and the Genoa area. I found myself in the iconic district of Navigli in Milan, where the sun rises high and brimming over canals and buildings and the beautiful romanesque basilica of Sant' Ambrogio, its 13th century mosaics, burial crypts and elegant columns are just a stone's throw away. Here, people ride about on bicycles, visitors sip Aperol, artists stravaig and scientists explore; students meet at *l'ora dell'aperitivo* for cheap eats. It was in this place, I saw a mother on a café terrace, clearly at a business meeting with an older man, breast-feeding her baby. The only person who turned to look was me, accustomed as I am, to Scottish prudishness and reserve. It was here, in the run-of-the-mill café, at Milano Centrale railway station, that I ate arancini... soft, green and melting... the best of my life. And here, that I saw two business men out for lunch being served this dish, typical of this northern area of Italy and which I am including as something special from the north!

500g trofie or similar pasta
150g green beans sliced on the slant
100g cooked, cubed potatoes
3/4 tbsp pesto

Fill your pasta pot up to 7/8 with water. When boiling, put the pasta into the pot.

When the pasta is almost cooked to your liking, (al dente or cooked through) add the green beans.

Bring back up to the boil and cook for another few minutes until the beans are soft.

Reserve one or two ladlefuls of the pasta water and drain the pasta mix.

Mix the beans, pasta, pesto, and cooked potatoes together, add enough of the reserved pasta water to loosen the pesto, and serve.

STUFFED PASTA SHELLS (CONCHIGLIONI RIPIENI)

For 4 people:
22 giant pasta shells

If paccheri al ragù di manzo is a triumphal fanfare, this dish, for which you can substitute a meat alternative, is the equivalent of a 500-strong mixed choir singing the finale of Beethoven's

9th symphony. It is indeed an 'Ode to Joy', worthy of the great Master himself.

The stages of preparation are similar to making a lasagne, except that you have to cook the pasta before stuffing it. Unlike lasagne where the pasta dominates, the fine, pliable giant pasta shells allow you to work them and fill them at will, and complement the rich blending of both a bold bolognese and a sumptuous béchamel; in this dish the sauces play the starring role, voices redolent and ringing with tomatoes, spices, a successful soffritto in harmony with a mellifluous béchamel. Although like the trofie, potato and green bean dish this dish is not from the south, such is its depth of flavour, its robustness, its drama, that I feel that it is more than deserving of a place in a book about the food of southern Italy.

BOLOGNESE SAUCE

For 4 people:
3 carrots finely chopped
2 sticks celery finely chopped
1 onion very finely chopped
1 leek finely chopped
500g minced beef or vegetarian equivalent
1 tbsp tomato purée
4 cloves chopped garlic
2 cans peeled tomatoes
1 cup white wine
2 tsp fennel seeds
salt and pepper to taste
olive oil, enough to very thinly cover the base of the cooking pot
grated parmesan

Put the olive oil in the pot to heat and then brown the onion and the beef or equivalent.

Add the tomato purée and cook on a high flame for a few seconds.

Add the carrots, leek, garlic, fennel seeds and celery.

Cook for a few minutes, stirring from time to time, until the vegetables have softened a little.

Add the white wine, turn up the heat and cook for a few minutes to allow the alcohol to evaporate.

Add the tomatoes and a can full of hot water.

Bring everything to the boil and then turn the heat down to a simmer.

Cook for at least an hour or until the sauce has turned colour and has a coating sauce consistency.

Check for taste and season.

When the bolognese is ready set it aside.

Cook the pasta according to packet instructions.

Line the bottom of a roasting dish with a thin layer of sauce.

Fill each shell with bolognese sauce and arrange the pasta in the roasting tin.

BÉCHAMEL SAUCE

200g unsalted butter
200g flour
240ml whole milk
salt and nutmeg to taste (I don't always include nutmeg)

Melt the butter in a pot.

Add the flour slowly, integrating it with the butter.

When fully integrated remove the pot from the heat.

Begin adding the milk stirring continually to avoid lumps.

When the mixture begins to look like a runny sauce, return to the heat.

Stir continually until the mixture coats the back of a spoon but is not solid.

Remove from the heat and season.

It will continue to cook for a few minutes.

When the béchamel is cooked, pour it over the pasta mixture.

Sprinkle the parmesan over the contents of the dish and place in a hot oven.

Cook for 20–30 minutes or until the mixture is bubbling and the cheese has browned. Serve immediately.

A variation of this dish is to omit the béchamel sauce, creating an altogether lighter dish. When you have filled the conchiglioni with bolognese, dot cubes of mozzarella around the filled shells, sprinkle a generous amount of parmesan over the whole side and place in the oven. The result will bring gasps from your guests.

PASTA AND BEAN STEW VITICUSO STYLE (PASTA E FAGIOL' ALLA VITICUSAR)

This is an iconic dish from the south of Italy, a dish that comes from Italy's stout heart. It is a food that sustains, gives health and fuel for hard work or hard times. It is comforting in winter and a treat on a New Year's night. Pasta e fagiol' comes from the home. If it should appear on a restaurant menu as a special feature, I applaud the chef. Its roots are *la cucina povera,* simple, basic and unfussy, A food from the land and from larders, created with few ingredients. Pasta e fagiol' roots us, reminds us of where we came from, conjures up grandmothers, aunts and godmothers, stories of travel and arrival, of *gl' chioghere* (the clogs they walked in), of sewn linen bags, strung across the chest, containing the little they owned; of money sewn into underwear, and of *gle'zampogne,* (double chantered pipes).

Pasta e fagiol' is the music of Abruzzi, Lazio, Molise and southwards, often served at village fairs, saints' Feast Days and weddings. Pasta e fagiol' is the food of poets; food you want to dwell in... legacy, a confidence, a secret, passed down from mother to daughter. So lowly has been its status, so raw some of its history, that it was never talked about or served to anyone but immediate family.

Rachel Roddy, in sharing a recipe for readers of the Saturday *Guardian*, has raised its profile and status.

Here is my recipe. The finished dish is a flowing, silky medley of textures with the beans and the pasta combining to take pulpy and mild-flavoured centre stage. I am not a fan of maccheroni, however, although I have suggested using ditalini, as is traditional; in this case, maccheroni is a very worthy alternative. Their hollowness holds the thick, stewy soup very well.

> *1 large leek very finely chopped*
> *1 brown onion very finely chopped*
> *2 celery sticks finely chopped*
> *2 large carrots finely chopped*
> *6 cloves garlic finely chopped*
> *2 tins beans (borlotti is traditional, but cannellini or haricot will do equally well; pre-cooked chickpeas will also do)*
> *2 tins peeled tomatoes*
> *100g small pasta (ditalini are usual or large pasta broken up; even a mix of what's left in packets around your cupboard will work very well)*
> *salt and pepper*
> *1 tsp fennel seeds*

1 tsp sugar or honey
1 tsp chilli or hot smoked paprika are optional additions

In a large pot, sauté the onions until they turn golden and then add the leek, celery, carrots and garlic.

Turn down the heat to the lowest setting and sweat the vegetables until they are completely broken down.

Add the drained beans, the peeled tomatoes. Fill the empty tins with hot water, swirl them around and then add the water to your pot. Stir the ingredients together, add the dry spices if using and cook for at least an hour or until everything is combined and well cooked.

Take out a large cupful of the mixture, purée it to thicken, and then mix the purée back into the pot. The basis of the soup is now ready. At this point you may want to add flavour... honey or sugar, fresh oregano or marjoram.

Ten minutes before you wish to serve, put the pasta into mix and let it cook through.

The dish should look more like a stew than a soup.

Serve with a mixed salad and a rough bread or homemade focaccia.

This dish improves with the keeping and can be very successfully reheated the next day.

For a non-vegetarian variation, add bacon lardons or pancetta after you have sautéed the onions and before adding the rest of the vegetables.

Another variation is to chop all the vegetables into bite-sized chunks; cook in the same order as the original, add the beans and tomatoes and cook until the vegetables become soft and break up. Then add the pasta. This will result in a chunkier dish.

ORZO WITH PESTO AND HAZELNUTS
(ORZO AL PESTO CON NOCCIOLE)

Recently, I was putting together a small buffet for two friends who were coming to visit. I wanted to add pasta without making it a centrepiece. I decided to use orzo which I think is too often diminished to, at best, a salad ingredient or alternatively, a mere rice or potato side dish.

As a pasta dish in its own right, orzo is without drama, gentle, subtle and undemanding, yet capable of holding its own as a starter dish or a light supper, with the thoughtful, sympathetic addition of a few extra textures and flavours; just enough to complement it.

Served at room temperature, coated in a zesty, lively green pesto, with halved and broken hazelnuts and creamy, curled ribbons of parmigiano or pecorino, maybe with a slice of lemon, orzo can be your easy-cook best friend. Pesto is an ideal sauce, colouring and flavouring, without overwhelming, these delicate, unassuming little grains.

SPAGHETTI WITH A GARLIC AND OLIVE OIL SAUCE
(SPAGHETTI ALL'AGLIO E OLIO)

When the cupboards are bare, when you are low in energy, when time is short, when the budget won't stretch much further, look no further than this tasty and simplest of all dishes.

I saw pasta all'aglio e olio many times as a child. It was sometimes eaten as described, pasta mixed with olive oil and raw garlic. The dish can be adapted of course, the garlic could be sautéed to reduce its bite. The choice of a green-flecked first-pressing oil, would make the dish look spectacular. My grandma sometimes added a few tinned anchovy fillets if she had some; or more often, some grated parmesan cheese. Anchovies go so well with long pasta such as spaghetti, tonnarelli from Lazio or fettucine. Small richly brown slivers together with the melting creaminess of a good cheese such as pecorino or gran padano in and among loosely folded strands, cannot fail.

This dish often makes us want to eat, even when we don't need to, is food that looks so good, it is impossible to resist. (It is surely the dizzying combination of texture and colour, displaying all the dish might offer, that seduces reason, taste buds and willpower).

Like pasta cacio e pepe from Rome and the South, pasta all'aglio e olio is again *la cucina povera* at work and at its most authentic.

The secret of the dish is not to spare the olive oil and to use the best variety you can obtain.

And to Drink

Every pasta dish has its own character – some are more substantial than others; some are meat based, others are light and vegetable based. Some can act as a main course, others as a light prelude. For these reasons, I suggest different wine-pairings.

With the ragù napoletano (or ragù di manzo), a rich, heavy sauce, a hearty, vibrant red is called for. A Primitivo from Puglia or more unusually, a Nero di Troia from the same region, soft, silky with just the right amount of acidity. Also from nearby regions, a Bombino Nero or Bombino Bianco, excellent wines and yet to be discovered by the wider wine drinking world would match well.

For sugo di pomodori freschi, a light tomato sauce, a light fruity white goes best, such as one of my old time favourites, a Frascati from Lazio which is mainly produced with the Malvasia grape. You will be captivated by its 'intense, distinctive, perfumed and delicate scent, and dry, soft, comfortable, inviting and elegant taste' (italianwine.guide).

The sugo di pomodori, a medium to rich sauce, calls for something red, robust and full flavoured, like a majestic Montepulciano from the Abruzzi. If you prefer a white, a classic Pecorino is light, dry and mineral. It is a wine with character and will accompany a sugo superbly.

For the trofie, try the amazing Greco di Tufo, a white wine from Campania. This is an intense white, full-bodied and with a slightly bitter aftertaste.

Pasta e fagiol' alla Viticusar needs a robust red such as some of those mentioned above. A Montepulciano d'Abruzzo would be my first choice. After that, a rich Primitivo from Puglia. There are so many Primitivo available, it is worth paying a little more to get the best quality.

La cucina povera

Music

'Viva la pappa col pomodoro' sung by Rita Pavone
No Solo Nostalgia, 1995

'A pizza' sung by Aurelio Fierro
Le Canzoni Classiche di Napoli, 2014

MY CHILDHOOD MEMORIES are mainly of our Bruntsfield kitchen… large stock pots filled with herbs, onions and floating chunky bones. The meaty, gentle delight of bone marrow fed to me on a teaspoon, was a delicacy which my cousins and I would fight over. And the sheer bliss of fatty, salty crackling! More challenging were the brown, stringy, chicken necks which we would gnaw at, trying to find something edible between the bones and gristle; and Grandma eating the hen's tail-end, which I once attempted to eat too.

There are so many stories in recipe books, food articles and online, by Italians recalling the pastina in brodo of their childhood. It is a simple, easy soup of broth and pasta, of *nonna, nini, nana, mammina, grammi, mimi* or however we called our Italian grandmothers, head of the household and the heart and stay of the family. This dish evokes a soft, warm bosom, a place to run to, a place to heal, to be spoiled and a home of pots and purées, of smells and surprises and the most loving smiles. What pleased my Grandma most was to see us eat up and polish the plate. In that moment, we were her pride and joy. To feed me back to health when I wasn't well and more generally to make sure that through her food I became robust and healthy, was her main focus. So, *magne'mamma, ca te fa' ross'!* (Eat and you'll grow up healthy!)

Brodo (broth or stock)

Stock-making very much depends on what you have to hand but here are a few basic recipes I use.

VEGETABLE STOCK

Chop very finely 2 carrots, 2 sticks of celery, 2 onions and 1 leek and soften in olive oil in a large pot.
Add garlic and brown.

Pour in 1–2 litres of water, bring to boiling and cook on a very low heat until the vegetables are soft and the stock has reduced. Liquidise everything in the pot with a stick blender.

The brodo is ready for the addition of pastina and any vegetable or herb you wish to include.

Another approach to making stock is to store in a large pot, over a few days, all the discarded bits from any vegetables you have used to cook. Wash them thoroughly, add water and any seasoning and herbs you fancy. The stock is ready when the vegetables are soft and cooked through. Strain the broth and use or let it cool and freeze it for future use.

CHICKEN STOCK

Put a whole chicken, without giblets, into a large pot of water. Bring to the boil and cook the chicken, which you can serve separately or use later.

Strain the stock until you have a clear liquid, let it cool and place in the fridge.

The following day, remove any fat which has gathered on the surface.

The stock is now ready for you to add other ingredients.

BEEF STOCK

Ask the butcher for 2kg of meaty beef bones for stock, some veal bones and 500g of stewing steak in one piece.

Put these into a roasting tin along with 2 carrots, an onion, 2 sticks of celery, a bay leaf, a handful of thyme, 4 cloves of garlic and the washed, discarded bits of any vegetables you have used for another dish.

Add a generous amount of olive oil and cook everything in an oven at 200–250°C until browned.

Place the contents of the roasting tin into a large stock pot.

Scrape the roasting tin and add all the bits and pieces to the pot and cover with water.

Bring to the boil and then lower the heat to the very minimum. Keep skimming the stock to remove fat, taking care not to stir.

After 2–3 hours, strain the broth and remove all the solids.

The steak can be reserved for another dish… as an addition to a pasta for instance, served on the side.

Pour the stock through a tea towel or muslin into another container and cool before placing in the fridge or using.

PASTINA (SMALL PASTA FOR SOUP)

Below is a list of small pasta, or pastina, generally used for soups. The list is by no means exhaustive, comprehensive or prescriptive:

- alfabettini – alphabet shapes
- ditali – short pasta tubes
- ditalini – tiny pasta tubes
- stelline – star shaped pasta, holes in the middle
- stellette – bigger stars with holes in the middle
- farfalline – small butterfly shapes
- risoni – rice shaped pasta, a bit like orzo
- cubotti – cube-like tubes
- anelletti – pasta rings
- passatelli – speciality pasta made with breadcrumbs, eggs and cheese, like corkscrews
- vermicelli – very thin pasta strands

PASTINA IN A BROTH (PASTINA IN BRODO)

1 or 2 cups of any short pasta depending on how thin or thick you prefer your soup
a handful of spinach, cavolo nero or any green vegetable, very finely chopped
parsley or another fresh herb of choice, finely chopped
grated parmesan cheese, or similar

Add any short pasta, and or any chopped vegetable to your stock.

Cook everything until soft.

Ladle the soup into deep bowls and sprinkle with grated cheese, chopped herbs and a lick of virgin olive oil.

STRACCIATELLA

chicken stock
1 egg
parsley or other herb

Bring a potful of chicken stock to the boil.

Whisk the egg and pour it gradually into the pot.

Stir the mixture until the egg has dispersed a little.

Add chopped parsley, sage or rosemary and finish with grated parmesan or similar.

You may also want to add a finely chopped leafy green vegetable and a handful of short pasta.

Picchiapò

In 2018, #*tavoleromane* launched a monthly dialogue and created an online meeting forum based on the keynotes of Roman cookery. The online narrative described the basic principles of Roman cooking and a food philosophy that applied throughout the region: '*In primis la pratica del riusa; la cucina romanesca, in quanta cucina povera, si serviva del genio casalinga per trasformare al meglio ingredienti semplici a di scarti e riciclare invece quelli più rari e pregiati*' (Roman cooking takes its inspiration from the vision and skill of home cooks, transforming simple, basic ingredients, or food that you might discard and making the best use possible of what is hard to come by or expensive to buy.) These principles – *la cucina povera* – are fundamental to the food of Rome.

One of the great triumphs of the Scottish kitchen must surely be stovies, a delicious re-presentation of beef and roast potatoes left over from Sunday's roast. The triumphant blending of onions, potatoes, and strands or chunks of beef with fat, is devilishly moreish. To be offered homemade stovies in a Scottish home is, like homemade pasta, both a rare treasure and a compliment. Like many of the dishes in this book, stovies are a fine legacy, a warm memory of love and care, a reconnection with family and history, of political and economical struggle too and a wistful reflection on another time, of parents and play and the carefree rough and tumble of siblings. While my grandma was in the scullery of our tenement flat, with its bed recess and coal fire, the aromas of garlic, parsley and tomatoes melting in the pot wafted through the doorway to the common stair. I have no doubt that in some other flat nearby, another grandmother, would be in the throes of her own particular way with stovies for her family. '*Necessitá fa virtú*' (Necessity is the mother of invention').

The recipes I have chosen to include in this book are mainly vegetarian because they are what I enjoy cooking best for friends and family. I also want to showcase the vast range of vegetarian dishes to be discovered in Italy's South. However, such is the current momentum in Italy and elsewhere, for reclaiming ancient traditions, a shout to legacy, lineage, culture and even our old languages, that I have decided to share this humble dish using leftover meat.

Picchiapò is our Italian equivalent of stovies, using cooked beef. It is mainly enjoyed in wintertime as part of the Christmas season and possibly takes its name from either *picchiare* (to pick at) or *piccante* (spicy). In the spirit of *la cucina povera,* the dish is increasingly to be seen now on menus in fashionable, on-trend areas of Rome. Also, since the dish is brodo based, I feel it has a place here.

PICCHIAPÒ

1kg boiled beef
a cup of beef stock
250g small tomatoes quartered
a few chopped carrots
400g chopped onions
1 whole stick of chopped celery including leaves
3 or 4 cooked potatoes cut into small cubes
2 cloves of minced garlic
a splash of red wine

Shred the cold cooked beef.

In a shallow pan, sauté the onions until they caramelise, then add the carrots, garlic and celery and finally the potatoes.

Cook until everything is softened.

Pour in the red wine and boil for a minute or two, then add

the tomatoes and the beef broth.

Lower the heat to simmer, add the beef and cook until the contents of the pan are reduced and you have a rich stew.

UOVA AL SUGO DI POMODORO

One of my favourite breakfasts and an absolute treat is shashuka, popular in North Africa, Turkey, Greece and the Middle East. There are many variations but the dish consists essentially of eggs in a spicy tomato sauce, often with onions, peppers, leeks, mushrooms and even avocados added. Various flavourings include cumin, harissa, paprika, chilli and cayenne pepper.

Southern Italy, Sicily and Sardinia each have their own versions, probably dating as far back as Muslim rule in the 9th century and subsequent invasions throughout the Middle Ages.

This recipe makes a wonderfully light dinner especially after a weekend of over-indulgence, when you need to be kind to your innards and spare the calories. It requires very little effort and you will probably already have all you need to hand.

> Serves 2–4 people:
> 4 *eggs*
> 2 *cloves of chopped garlic*
> 1 *tbsp tomato purée*
> 1 *litre passata*
> *olive oil*
> 1 *tsp mild smoked paprika and any other spice of your choice*
> *a handful of parsley and chives*

In a wide pan, sauté the garlic in the olive oil.
Add the tomato purée and cook briefly.
Add the spices.

Pour in the passata and bring everything to the boil.

Reduce the heat and cook for about 20 minutes or until the sauce has thickened.

Drop in each of the eggs and poach them gently until cooked.

When the eggs are set remove from the heat and scatter over the herbs.

Spoon each egg in its sauce into a bowl and serve with a chunk of lightly toasted bread.

A HEARTY SOUP (LA MINESTRA)

My most memorable food moments from my annual stravaiging through the Highlands and the Scottish isles are, on balance, soups. Soups from home kitchens in community centres where my heart skips a beat at watching local people congregate, hearing the soft, fey Gaelic tongue or a tune from a set of small pipes. Soup gloriously thick, green or velvety and golden. Or steaming broths, crammed full of goodies and elevated to full meal status, with the addition of barley, red lentils and split peas, best when the slice of bread at your elbow, maybe two, is chunky, thick and tasty enough not to require any butter. These soups served by kindly women are foodie heaven. They soothe with their warmth and they are the best barrier I can think of, against the summer chill when your very bones have shivered and shrunk in a 4-season sleeping bag at 2am on an August morn, a gale blowing everything down and threatening to take you with it out to sea.

The same *paesano* or home kitchen culture applies around una minestra whether it be in Rome's Trastevere, the Val Porcina or in a local Cassino *osteria*. Minestra is a vegetable broth. In Italian homes, a minestra, with good fresh ingredients is still seen as the way to good health, to recovery, to comfort, and to ensuring that the family is well nourished.

Cheese is always added for protein, body and flavour.

Minestrone in Italian means a large minestra... a grand soup or broth, from the time of ancient Rome. It was a food for labourers, servants and those who worked hard for their rich masters and their families. There is plenty scope here for invention and using what you have, leftovers included. Add rice, cannellini or borlotti beans, orzo, and even a much more substantial short pasta like malfatti, maltagliati, cavatappi and minestra becomes a meal.

Southern Italian style cooking has travelled far and wide and the iconic, exported minestrone that most of us recognise, is red because of the addition of sweet, juicy tomatoes. However, in Liguria and around that area, minestrone is often not what you might expect and is green rather than red. Sometimes now when I have guests, I make two minestroni: a traditional one with tomatoes and a green minestrone. There is something purifying and cleansing about this alternative minestrone and I hope you will try it and enjoy its freshness.

GREEN MINESTRONE (MINESTRONE ALLA LIGURE)

vegetable stock
1 brown onion finely chopped
3 leeks chopped
2 sticks celery
1 small fennel bulb, leaves included, finely chopped
the stalks of cavolo nero, finely chopped
2 cloves garlic
olive oil
150g rigatoni corti or any short pasta of your choice, or rice
1 cup beans: cannelloni, haricot or butter
a splash of lemon juice
a few leaves of marjoram or oregano
parmesan or pecorino or fontina cheese grated to taste
salt and pepper

Cook the onion until golden.

Add the garlic, leeks, celery stalks and fennel.

Cook for a few minutes and then add the stock and any combination of the following:

1 cup broad or fava beans if in season
100g French beans topped and tailed and cut diagonally
1 cup fresh or frozen peas
cavolo nero, leaves roughly chopped
4 courgettes, chopped
1 savoy cabbage, chopped into short strips

When everything is cooked, blitz a cupful of the soup and pour it back into the pot.

Then add the pasta or rice.

When cooked through, serve.

Once bowls are filled, top with parmesan or pangrattato and hand round a bowl of pesto.

> Tip: You can use a pangrattato on any dish including pasta, risotto or polenta. It will work equally well on a pizza and is delicious on baked or roasted fish or to finish a plate of sautéed greens.

PAPPA OR PAPPOCCE'

This recipe for pappocce' comes from my cousin Angela. She is a legendary, noteworthy businesswoman on the Fylde coast in Lancashire; feisty, funny and always glamorous. She once considered using the name of this dish for one of her restaurants but decided its pronunciation, in a mainly Lancashire accent, might challenge her clientèle just a little too much. My visits to Lytham St Annes to see her are a tonic for my soul and for my psyche. We laugh a lot, often at ourselves and life in general. I leave her feeling loved and full of joy.

Like most of the dishes from southern Italy, and from our family closets, the recipe is another excellent example of getting the very best from every ingredient, wasting nothing and using whatever you have in the fridge in order to make a nourishing and tasty meal. Olive oil and garlic are the key ingredients and if you always have these to hand, and maybe a stray tomato or two, you will always make something tasty.

1 cup of sugo
2–3 slices stale bread
1 litre stock
a handful of chopped uncooked vegetables (whatever you have)
salt and pepper

Very finely chop whatever uncooked vegetables you have.

Sauté them with 2 cloves of chopped garlic.

When everything is almost cooked add the sugo, the bread and the stock.

Cook everything until you have something between the consistency of a soup and a pudding.

Add some fresh herbs.

Season well and enjoy your supper.

The recipe can be adapted to make use of leftover cooked vegetables, which are chopped and added with the bread to the liquids in the pot.

If all else fails, a bag of frozen peas works beautifully with the garlic, olive oil and sweet, pulpy, tomatoey bread.

For a basic pappa, combine the liquids, stock and sugo, add a quantity of small pasta and serve with torn basil leaves and some grated cheese.

RISOTTO

Signora B was a fine lady of poise, great courtesy and refinement. Her floral dresses of silk, cut to both envelop and define her full figure, gave her the air of someone of noble descent, as did her proud gait. She wore red lipsticks which evoked glamour and ruby vermouths, low-toned gatherings in cloisters and great historic halls formed of Brunelleschi geometric architecture and filled with Renaissance art work; fine music, Corelli or Gaudioso perhaps, playing in the background.

From *la signora*, I learned about the refreshing qualities of chilled tea with slices of lemon to counter the searing heat of a Florentine summer. I also learned about an Italy that was as foreign to me, culturally and linguistically, as a trip through the Rhine Valley with a party of Norwegians. This Italy, not one I recognised, was one of quiet manner and containment; an Italy of discreet tailoring and soft, well-cut leather shoes, where restive men rapidly drank their morning espresso standing at the bar and in the late afternoon, well turned out ladies met in tea salons and politely ate cake.

For five months, while I attended the *universita per stranieri*, I rented a modest, traditionally furnished room from Signora B which overlooked the river Arno. In order to pay my rent, I gave English lessons twice a week and I learned to tie beautiful bows and apply ribbons to carefully wrapped parcels containing quality leather handbags, which I sold to the rich ladies of the city. All in a manner appropriate to an iconic leather boutique, owned by Signora B's son, who made it clear that if I offered other services, I might earn some more. I am glad to report I did not. I did, however, secure a boyfriend, which offered some protection from male predators and I worked contentedly in that shop every afternoon for all of the time I was in Florence.

As I had no cooking facilities and was living on a meagre income, I usually ate my modest evening meal – all I could afford was a plate of pasta and a Coca Cola – in a small restaurant a few doors down from where I lived. It was there that I tasted risotto for the first time.

Risotto was not a dish of my childhood but as I later became increasingly interested in cooking, I learned to make it for my family. The technique is easy, provided that you use the right rice. This is essential, since these grains of rice, generally arborio or carnaroli, firm and creamy when cooked, release their starch into the broth creating a sumptuous, soft yet grainy, elegant dish flavoured by a clever pairing of vegetables, with some sage leaves, or oregano, and a dash of lemon juice. A word of warning: beware a menu that boasts 'creamy risotto'. If the right rice is used, there is no need to add cream. Cream, apart from being inauthentic, certainly for a southerner, only makes the dish cloying and indigestible. The mantecato – grated parmesan and a knob of butter which is added just before serving – is the final traditional flourish and provides all the creaminess you need.

Risotto is a dish which requires time and constant attention while it cooks. Whether you choose arborio or carnaroli or a vialone nano rice depends on the result you want to achieve. Here is the reason that Italian risotto rice is essential and nothing else will do. Arborio is high in starch and yields a silkiness. When the mantecato is added, the glow and softness of the starchy mix, studded with flakes of fish, clams or prawns, nuggets of vegetables and/or spicy choice meats, Italian sausage perhaps or 'nduja, a spreadable Calabrian sausage, is mouth-watering. Carnaroli rice is less creamy and like vialone nano rice, holds its shape, so that unlike a risotto of arborio rice which slides off the spoon, and which you can swallow in a mighty gulp, your every taste bud thrumming, the Carnaroli or vialone nano risotto, like barley, is more grainy and satisfyingly chewy.

Risottos *al bianco* are traditional in the north of Italy and though I find them less remarkable in terms of taste, compared to the food of the South, I do admit to enjoying a smoked haddock risotto with peas and lemon juice. It is a dish that is smoky, salty yet deliciously sweet. Lemon juice, only a touch, adds another layer of flavour and brings out the combined flavours of toasted rice, fish and peas.

Any risotto eaten in Naples or around, will probably contain fish or seafood which works so well with tomatoes: risotto al pomodoro as an example, is very popular: risotto cooked in a sugo of tomatoes, with calamari and a dressing of ricotta, olive oil, parsley and lemon juice added towards the end of the cooking time. More recently however, as well as dishes with a more southern twist, using the ingredients typical of the south of Italy, I have experimented with ingredients from other Mediterranean countries.

RISOTTO WITH SMOKED HADDOCK AND PEAS (RISOTTO DI PESCI E PISELLI)

1 onion chopped
300g risotto rice
1 cup white wine
3 cloves of smashed and finely chopped garlic
1 or 2 smoked haddock fillets cut into smallish chunks
a handful of frozen peas
1 1/4 litres of vegetable stock
olive oil
black pepper
sage or oregano leaves chopped or torn, to serve

In a shallow pan, sauté the onion until golden.

Add garlic and fry until the smell of garlic rises.

Add the rice and toast it, turning constantly for about 2–3 minutes.

Add the wine and cook vigorously until the alcohol evaporates.

Then pour in half the stock and add the fish.

Stir the contents of the pan continuously.

Keep adding stock, as much as you need, and tasting and seasoning the rice.

When the rice is almost cooked, add the peas.

Cook for a minute longer.

The risotto is ready when it resembles a thick soup.

Season with pepper.

Remove from the heat and stir in the mantecato (a handful of grated parmesan and a tablespoon of butter).

Decorate with some chopped sage or oregano and bring to the table.

RISOTTO WITH MUSHROOMS AND BLACK OLIVES (RISOTTO ALLA ROMANA)

This is a satisfyingly rich dish of strong, earthy flavours. There is a dark-heartedness to it. Like the music of Rome, the tarantella, the pipes, accordions, and other free-reed instruments, and the guttural southern languages, this dish evokes straightforward rawness. Garlic and onion are a base which serve to coax the key ingredients to give up their best.

1 onion chopped
3 cloves of garlic finely chopped
250g chestnut mushrooms, skinned or skin on and cleaned, cut vertically into 2 or 3 slices

6 black olives, stoned and cut in half
300g risotto rice
1 cup white wine
1 tin chopped tomatoes
1 1/4 litres of chicken or vegetable stock

In a shallow pan, sauté the onion until golden.

Add the finely chopped garlic and the mushrooms.

Cook until they have taken on colour.

Add the rice and toast briefly for 2–3 minutes.

Add the wine and cook vigorously until the alcohol evaporates.

Add the peeled tomatoes.

Rinse the empty tin with boiled water and add it to the pan.

Turn over the contents.

Start adding stock and keep stirring until the rice is almost cooked.

Finally, add the olives.

When you have what looks like a thick soup, add the mantecato and serve.

You could replace the mantecato with a drizzle of olive oil and a tablespoon of ricotta and mix these through before spooning out the risotto.

You could also add some roasted cherry tomatoes before serving which will explode in your mouth, adding some smokey sweetness, and will give another layer of moisture to the richness of the dish.

RISOTTO WITH AUBERGINES, BASIL AND FETA
(RISOTTO ALLE MELANZANE CON BASILICO E FETA)

1 onion sliced very thinly
4 cloves of crushed garlic
1 cup of sugo
2 medium sized aubergines sliced thinly on the slant
300g arborio or carnaroli rice
150g feta cheese crumbled
1 cup white wine
1¼ litres of chicken or vegetable stock
the rind of a block of parmesan cheese (this is an easy and economical way to add flavour to a dish)
a handful of chopped basil

This recipe is an effective way of using up any leftover sugo or some of your stockpile from the freezer.

Heat the oven to 220°C and lay all the sliced aubergines on a well oiled oven tray. Turn them over once and cook until they are slightly scorched. This should take about 15 minutes.

Put 2 tablespoons of olive oil in a wide shallow pan and sauté the onions until golden then add the garlic.

When the aroma of garlic rises, add the rice and briefly toast.

Pour in the wine and turn up the heat. Let it bubble for a few seconds and then add the sugo, the aubergines and the chunk of parmigiano rind.

Keep turning over the contents of the pan and gradually add the stock.

Keep adding stock until the rice is cooked through and the mixture resembles a thick soup. Add the chopped basil.

Turn off the heat, add the crumbled feta cheese and serve.

You may want to add a squeeze of lemon before taking the dish to the table.

RISOTTO WITH BEETROOT, MINT AND GOATS CHEESE (RISOTTO ALLA BARBIETOLA CON FORMAGGIO DI CAPRA)

Any strong cheese such as gorgonzola, crema di dolcelatte, taleggio or goats cheese will work well with this dish.

2 medium fresh cooked beetroot, chopped
2 cloves of chopped and crushed garlic
150g creamy goats cheese or another cheese of your choice, crumbled
300g risotto rice
1 cup white wine
1 1/4 litres of chicken or vegetable stock
a handful of chopped mint
juice of half a lemon

In a wide, shallow saucepan sauté the garlic in olive oil.

Add the rice and toast until every grain has been in contact with the oil.

Add the white wine and let it bubble for several seconds.

Add the beetroot and a little stock and then keep adding stock until the mixture is cooked through but loose.

Stir though the cheese or cheeses, add lemon juice and top with mint.

Serve immediately.

Polenta

Many countries write songs about *la mamma* and depending on the culture, the songs are sung with varying degrees of emotion or restraint. Kenny Ball's *My Mother's Eyes* (recorded in 1961) will surely bring a lump to your throat. Sophie Tucker's Yiddish version is even more poignant. Italy is unashamedly and maybe uniquely, a place where love for a mother is expressed with a passion somewhat akin to what in other countries might be reserved for a lover only. There is no shame in this. People identify with it. They cry with it. They melt at any sign of it. Mother love is part of a culture; a national characteristic. Mothers may even take precedence over muttering, sighing wives, ultimately resigned and silent. No winning that battle. But some consolation might yet be found in their sons whom they glorify, who adore them in equal measure, and who usually continue, throughout their lives, to behave as 'glorified' individuals. There was an occasion when Claudio Villa, four times winner of the Sanremo Song Festival in the '50s and '60s, broke down on stage while singing *Mamma*. For a few moments, in front of a large audience he stepped back, unable to continue. In the gap that followed, the backing music played on, the singer stood with his hand to his bowed head, suddenly with a roar, the audience rose to its feet, crying and clapping at the same time. The singer recovered, the audience completely with him, and he ended the song to an uproar of tearful, smiling applause.

Italy must surely be exceptional too in the number of songs that exist about food... songs about pizza for instance... about the girlfriend who whenever she went out, whether to fine dining restaurants, or indeed when choosing her wedding cake, insisted on demanding nothing but pizza '*colla pomarola n'goppe*' (topped with tomatoes). Songs about fried fish, maccheroni; baccalà, coffee, pasta and bread. In fact I cannot think of any other country that sings so much and so warm-heartedly about food and about *la mamma*. It tells us a lot about southern Italians in particular, about their irresistable charm; and it says something about the delightful child within. It also tells us that *la mamma* for any Italian means good food and home. The messages on menus throughout the South abound… 'food as mamma made it'… and in Mimmo our Pugliese host's words, spoken with breathy reverence, as he prepared frittelle on our AirBnB terrace: '*la ricetta di mia madre*' (the recipe is my mamma's). Nothing else for it but to bow our heads.

Some foods just make us feel warm and wonderfully coddled. While pasta for me would possibly dominate those thoughts of home, polenta is an equal contender as a staple, and for many, a food of childhood. Its effect may be rather like that of Irish stew, the humble egg and chips or rice pudding. Polenta is the food of country, of agrarian communities dispersed across the Po valley and the rice fields of the North. Prepared northern style, polenta is creamy with melted cheese and butter, topped with the woody crush of porcini mushrooms. It may be served with fish or presented with a wild boar stew on the side; or indeed merely topped with truffles. In the South, the approach is quite different. In Naples, Bari and Puglia scagliozzi are a popular street food. The cooked cornmeal porridge is spread on a flat surface, flattened with a rolling pin and cut into chips which are then drizzled with olive oil, rock salt and baked for around 30 minutes with a generous sprinkling of parmesan or pecorino cheese. Or the creamed porridge is cut into large triangles, deep fried, and sold as a sumptuous street food from city pop-ups, topped with pancetta, guanciale or a suitable cheese such as provola.

The way I like it best though is polenta al sugo bathed and bubbling in a good rich tomato sauce, so sweet, so soft that nothing else is required. That is the way that I remember eating it for the first time, straight from the soup plate that Grandma put before me. And there can be no dish more comforting, more satisfying, than plunging your large spoon into a lush, velvety, deep bowl of polenta, redolent with tomatoes collapsing and oozing into the billowy mix, crowned with a melting layer of rough grated parmesan; and offset by a mix of grilled sweet peppers, mushrooms cooked with garlic and balsamic; or some sautéed greens on the side. This dish soothes and enfolds, it is *la ninna nanna* (think rocking songs!) of all dishes and leaves you feeling that you can sleep soundly because all is right in your world.

CLASSIC POLENTA (POLENTA AL SUGO DI POMODORO)

1 litre water
250g polenta
3 tbsp butter or olive oil
tomato sugo
homemade or shop-bought ricotta
fresh basil, sage or marjoram finely chopped
(optional sautéed greens)

Bring the water to a rolling boil.

Gradually add the polenta in a thin stream.

Keep whisking until the polenta is integrated and there are no lumps.

Lower the heat and gently stir the polenta with a wooden spoon until it has the consistency of porridge and the mixture comes away cleanly from the pan (you may need to add more water as you stir).

Stir in the butter (or olive oil).

Ladle into soup plates and top with the sugo, followed by a spoonful of ricotta.

Sprinkle with the herb of your choice.

Add sautéed greens on the side.

SCAGLIOZZI (STREET FOOD OF THE SOUTH)

Follow the recipe above until the polenta is cooked.

Pour the polenta on to a baking tray and using a rolling pin or a dough scraper to flatten the mixture to a depth of roughly 2 cm getting it as even as you can and leave to set.

Cut the set polenta into triangles, fingers, cubes, wedges or whatever shape you like.

Cook until golden in hot olive oil and serve immediately coupled with an Italian vermouth (red or a chilled white) and a slice of lemon or orange.

And to Drink

My choice for risotto or any polenta dish would be a light red. Frappato from Sicily is a perfect light to medium red. It works equally well served at room temperature or chilled. However, if white is preferred, a Chardonnay from Puglia would be excellent.

Ports, boats and Marechiaro

Music

'Marechiare' sung live by Claudio Villa
'E cchiù bell' canzone 'e Claudio Villa, 2006

'Chiaro di Luna' written and sung by Jovanotti
Smart Working Soundtrack, 2020

THE WAY TO find the real wonder of any city, town or neighbourhood, is to walk around it. In walking miles, we begin to notice what is intrinsic and different to what we know... how people look, how they dress and move around, how they sound; all of it tells a story.

For example, in the *barrios* of Argentina, in San Telmo at breakfast, I saw a couple tangoing on the street. The moment was theirs alone; no one turned to stare. In Hanoi I watched crowds of people, of all ages, by the Hoan Kiem Lake, gracing the early morning with the easy flow of Tai Chi. I also saw people resignedly picking their way through fallen trees, through parks and blocked doorways, trees brought down the previous night by the tornado which had killed several people in the city.

In Paris I watched an elegant grandmother, white hair held becomingly in a tortoiseshell clasp, delicately eating nougat glacé in the company of her chic (I assumed) grandson. He was fine boned, white shirted, with a dark mop of designer-cut hair. They captured, both in their dress and conversation, all that I understand about the people of Paris. I saw the same elegance of behaviour, economy of style, in the shops and on the pavements, in bistrots too, in the Faubourg St Honoré where I was lucky enough to eat a salade niçoise at a white tableclothed restaurant in the thrall of well-tailored suiting, Cacharel perfume and Jimmy Choo shoes.

In Costa Rica I saw men working the coffee plantations, no doubt for very little recompense. In Athens I sat among people meeting to eat a midnight dinner when the sun had well and truly turned its back and the day's heat had dimmed. There, I learned about love between friends demonstrated without reserve; I also learned about the symbolism in visual art and iconography.

And in San Diego, the strict protocols around alcohol in the USA, forced us, in order to get a sly cocktail for our 16- and 18-year-old daughters, to run the gauntlet of walking across the

Mexican border on foot and taking a taxi to Tijuana. There we drank cocktails by the yard and danced the night away. And travelling down through the pampas of southern Argentina, a gun in our host's glove compartment, and outside, men riding bareback in cowboy hats… all of these experiences gave me a whole new take on the world we live in.

A real priority for me is to explore food markets wherever I go. Malaga's *mercado central*, is magnificent. Strawberries big as red apples only more luscious. Creamy, crumbly, craggy cheeses… smooth and slick; grainy and granulated in wedges, cartwheels, and fat balls; some requiring only a spoon as a measure, others requiring something akin to a scythe-like action. Whole stalls of olives of every size and shade of black or green and a mottled fusion of both.

Roaming, observing, listening, the air heavy with wonderful aromas, we start to understand the importance of food in Spanish culture. Baskets overflowing with spices of every colour and hue, pungent scents of saffron and sweet paprika, earthy scents of cardamom, coriander, and ginger, nutty fragrances of sesame, all of these teach us the importance of spice, not only in Spanish cooking but in preparing food generally. The covered food halls of Arcachon in southwest France showcase the importance of sweet treats in French cuisine and the finesse and confection with which cakes, tarts and savoury puffs are made, exhibited and wrapped as a takeaway lunch.

The glory of Rome for me, is not so much the architectural majesty of that beautiful city, nor the history and trace of civilisations past, nor the wide, tree-lined streets, nor even leafy Lungotevere where you can meander with a long leisurely river for company. Rather, it is the daily thrum of life in Trastevere and Testaccio that provides the magic. These are the areas less visited, where people go and come, busy with the demands of the day, and lorries idle in narrow side streets. There the mind boggles at the impressive array of unctions and medicaments in local pharmacies, where serious, bespectacled staff offer attention and sober advice.

There you will spot barrow-loads of lettuces being hauled up a quiet street to some eatery or other, habit-clad nuns arm in arm gazing at a small statue of a madonna, haughty priests, proudly sporting heavy-chained crucifixes, whizzing bicycles with unlikely, oversized baggage or even the odd passenger or dog on handlebars; and small gatherings of people (men and *donne di casa* (homely women of a certain age) chatting outside the local bread shop as they wait to squeeze into the tiny space, where they have ten seconds to shout their order above the din.

To complete your experience, there may be a stylish but friendly corner breakfast/brunch place where you will see people eating a quick pizza slice, bright-eyed tourists surveying mounds of soft pasta on paper plates alongside workers and jacketed men having their morning latte with a cornetto con crema (custard filled croissants).

Marechiaro of course is famous. It is a small *borgo* (neighbourhood) of Naples where the blue, blue sea sparkles, dark Vesuvius darkly broods and the glorious, nearby islands of Capri, luscious Ischia and the shy, less glossy and therefore less visited Procida, beckon. The choice as to which one to visit when time is short, is hard, but I cannot forget Procida, where the clocks seemed to have stopped several decades ago. It was here we ate fresh anchovies for lunch and drank a characterful, chilled Vermentino by the water's edge. And in the stillness, the slow pace, everything closed in the heat of an October day except a few restaurants, it felt as though the rest of the world no longer existed and all was therefore well.

Naples' Marechiaro area, even today, even with buzzing E-scooters, grand hotels, bold street sellers and bustling pavements, is still romantic. Fishermen, skin cracked with the salt of seawater and a merciless sun, still fetch up here in sturdy old vessels among expensive yachts and industrial barges in the bay. And despite the chic, well-groomed Aperol drinkers and tourists that crowd the rows and rows of bars and seafood restaurants in the Borgo Santa Lucia, an authenticity still remains, to be savoured if you are alive to it. While most are inured to the traditional songs of Naples, known and endlessly played, the world over, I admit to being moved nonetheless. My blood rises, I feel the urge to hold out a hand, to the songsters and mandolinists singing the old songs I grew up with in the language of my grandmother. While early evening brings a mixed, vibrant, gathering, it is the early morning and a lone voice, a middle-aged man in a battered hat with a guitar, that makes me pause from walking to sit on the sea wall and listen, my throat dry.

In Naples, Cagliari, Gallipoli; in Catania, Bari and along Italy's glorious coastline from top to toe, there are fish markets a-plenty. Maybe the foremost of all, is the ancient fish market of Puglia. It is a bustling, thrilling fish emporium outside Bari's city walls. Like bouillabaisse in southern France, fish soup, an unpredictable delice of fish and seafood cooked in tomatoes… cacciucco in northern Livorno, brodetto on the Adriatic coast, u'bredette in the Molise and zuppa di pesci in Naples and the south, is a glorious celebration of the bounty of the seas that surround a country so blessed by nature. The story has it that fisherman used to prepare the dish with the leftovers that they couldn't sell. Having wrestled with the vagaries and uncertainties of the sea, their journeys and days perilous, this is how they repaid themselves and maybe still do. Zuppa di pesci is no less than a triumph of a dish, where tomatoes, white wine and garlic combine with the flavours of a superb array of fish and seafood.

FISH SOUP (ZUPPA DI PESCI)

I have so many memories of feasts around my table. In the centre, a cauldron no less, steaming and aromatic, out of which the pink scales of crustaceans poke upwards, oddly angular, in which claws and shells churn and bubble and creamy thick white flesh nestles. My kitchen is redolent with freshness and the tang of sea and its treasures. All of it awaits my ladle. My guests sit wide-eyed, excited, their bibs tied tightly, napkins and spoons poised, and I fill each bowl with a rich, fishy brew and as much shell and white fish as I can. It is the ensuing silence around the table that tells me I have succeeded; a silence interrupted by the hearty sounds of cracking shells, of sucking, and the sight of happy guests, cutlery abandoned as they wrestle tails, pincers and unyielding shells. I am not a regular visitor to my local fishmonger, but when I arrive, she brightens with anticipation of the tally at the end of my spree.

For a fish soup, southern Italian style, first make a tasty broth and then add any scallops (which take a little longer to cook), followed by whatever shell fish is available.

THE BROTH

3 or 4 cloves of garlic
olive oil
1 cup of white wine
2 tins chopped tomatoes
salt and pepper
juice of half a lemon
1 medium/large fillet of white fish roughly chopped

Start by finely chopping the garlic and sautéing in enough olive oil to cover the base of a very large, wide saucepan.

When the garlic starts to take on colour, add white wine and let it sizzle for a few seconds, until the alcohol has evaporated.

Add the chopped tomatoes.

Add about 2 tins of hot water to the pot. Stir well.

Turn up the heat.

Let the sauce boil for a few minutes then reduce to a simmer.

Cook for about 20 minutes to half an hour until you have a substantial tomato soup.

Add the white fish, let it break up and combine with the sauce in the pot. Add the lemon juice.

You now have a fish stock to which you will add more white fish and the seafood.

THE FISH

An assortment of the following:
crevettes, langoustines, prawns,
mussels, clams, scallops, crab claws,
lobster tails, salmon, swordfish, halibut

Wash all the shellfish very thoroughly.

For the mussels, remove the beards and brush the shells clean with a vegetable brush.

Once the broth is ready, add the fish and let it cook.

Add the shellfish, scallops first and then the rest.

Cover the pot for a very few minutes. Take care not to overcook the fish.

> Tip: When the mussels and clams have opened (discard any that are closed) and langoustines and prawns have turned pink, the zuppa is ready.

And to Drink

One of the greats from the southern region such as Fiano from Campania; floral, round and waxy; Falanghina which is medium bodied with aromas of honey and wild flowers; or the gorgeous Garganega, a lean, dry white which is lemony and has hints of honeydew melon and almonds.

La cucina di terra
'su mamma su' magne'
(eat it all up, my little one)

Music

'La canzone del pane' sung by I Camillas
Le Politiche del Prato, 2013

'Ciaccona' by Francesca Caccini (composer) sung by Elena Cecchi
Fedi and the choir of Cappella di Santa Maria degli Angeli
Caccini: Sacred and Secular Songs, 2013

DAY DAWNS FIERCELY in the South. Before the blazing arrival of sun, the landscape expectant, holds its breath as the pale stillness, mists and haze, succumb gradually to full daylight and the progress of hours. Time in southern Europe has a different colour and shape and day and night sound differently. In Athens traffic fumes, bustle and noise mark an entire city on the move: to work, to school, to daily routines and chores; then home, not once but twice a day. The midday meal and heat of summer define the day and the night. In southern Spain, and Italy, two countries I know well, it's the same.

In Rome and elsewhere in cities across the South, people of every occupation and profession – loose collared in suits, in hard hats, overalls, well-laundered jeans, many with quality and seasoned leather bags at their elbow – crowd local bars, stand shoulder to shoulder, at counters, agitatedly stirring espressos which they swallow in a gulp, or hastily downing caffè lattes together with a biscotto or a sweet pastry wrapped in paper. Café terraces are where those who take life at their ease watch the comings and goings, sitting in the morning sun which has not yet reached full strength. Southern Italians make little of breakfast – at most, a sweet pastry or a slice of bread with honey or butter.

In Pontemelfa in a modern villa, in the Frosinone region of Italy, where I am a guest, a house built with earnings brought back from the hard years Vincenzo spent working in Venezuela far from family, the house is stirring at 5.30 or 6am. There is the sound of a shower somewhere in the house. In the kitchen, the Moka coffee maker is gurgling. Vincenzo not fully dressed, but fresh and shaved, sits, in a white vest at the kitchen table. He is reading the *Gazzetta dello Sport* while his morning coffee percolates.

Slowly, the rest of the Pontemelfa household comes to life. The children, Chiarina and Luciano, pick up their *merenda,* a mid-morning snack, and leave for school. At midday they return with their father Vincenzo, gather in the kitchen anxious and very ready for lunch. It is the main event of the day. Everyone looks forward to lunch. Irena, Vincenzo's wife, has been to the local market for bread and whatever she needs for the main meal that day. After lunch, from about 2.30pm onwards everyone is asleep. We eat again at 9pm or even later, when the day has cooled and the air is fragrant with the aroma of ripening figs, grapes, lemons, walnuts. At last, there is freshness and a welcome, cool air. Tonight may not be too hot to sleep in comfort. Dinner is a light meal and often consists of a few leftovers from the day; maybe a panzanella salad, some fruit and pecorino cheese. A little local red wine served from recycled Coca Cola bottles, often mixed with water, is taken at both meals. For the children a little wine with lemonade. Usually, they are happier with a fizzy drink.

Not far from here, in Villa Latina Giovanni lives alone. He is almost 40 and to his mother's distress, without 'a wife'. He owns a dog and a gun. His simple, ancient stone house consists of two rooms. He never wears a shirt unless he is obliged to go to Rome to visit his bank or see a lawyer. Seen from the doorway of the house, his bedroom makes me think of a lair. Solidly masculine, there is something feral about him. Across the yard, his neighbour Antonietta emerges from more gloom. Her hair is completely white and cropped. Most of her teeth are missing. She looks at least 80 years old but is probably a lot younger. One eye is almost closed and the other does the job of two as it flits and jerks from earth to sky. She likes to chat, or rather to philosophise. And she regularly complains about the horrendous 'bouts of heat' of recent days – *'c'erte bafagne re call'*, she says in dialect. Either that, or she takes to swearing vengeance on a wrong doer – *'un' a me e cient' a te'* (for every wrong done to me, I will return it a hundredfold). Antonietta is fixed in my memory even after all these years. Fixed in memory too is the glorious panzanella I first ate there, more memorable than any other since. I watched as Giovanni's mother, Zi'Amelia, put large slabs of bread in a bowl and mixed them with roughly cut onions and large sweet tomatoes, all of which she dressed with copious amounts of local olive oil.

There are many recipes for panzanella. I usually use stale bread but you may prefer to toast yours or make croutons instead.

Feel free to vary the ingredients: hard-boiled eggs or anchovies are delicious; as are capers, cucumber, celery, fennel, sautéed pancetta, strips of prosciutto cotto or mortadella.

The salad may not look very beautiful but I assure you that your guests will request it again and again.

ROUGH BREAD SALAD (PANZANELLA)

4 slices stale, good quality bread cut into small squares
6 good sized tomatoes, cut in half horizontally and each half cut vertically into 2–3 sections but not slices
1 red onion very thinly sliced
1 clove garlic
a handful of fresh, stoned, green olives (optional)
olive oil
white wine vinegar
seasoning and basil, mint or any other herb to taste

Put the bread in a wide bowl.

Layer the tomatoes on top so that they soak the bread.

Add the onion, garlic and olives (if using).

Dress with a good glug of olive oil and a tablespoon of vinegar.

Leave to rest at room temperature and after at least an hour, turn over the contents of the bowl.

Leave for another half hour or more.

Turn everything over again and serve.

Beans, Pulses and Greens

There is so much philosophy and culture in certain ingredients. Beans and pulses are fundamental to life in the Meridionale, they are a staple in most homes, a complete meal in themselves. Lowly and unassuming, they offer a rich source of nutrition and are grown extensively from central to southern Italy.

For me, beans and pulses symbolise Italian resilience. It was that resilience that made them throw open their doors during the pandemic, and on balconies up and down the land, sing popular anthems of their past. In need of comfort and human contact, they inspired others to follow and like a rising storm, they faced down the terror that took and destroyed a world we had come to rely on. In corners and cities, they joined together in song and bold resistance. It is that resistance and resilience, an unflinching determination not to go under but to survive that exists in every Italian who has sought good fortune elsewhere. These qualities live on too, in those hardy folk who have remained in a land that often yields too little.

I will not forget those stirring scenes of solidarity. Like these memories, lentils and beans of every description 'take me home'. Usually presented in soups or salads, they were a strong feature of my childhood and life in our Bruntsfield flat. Partnered with tinned tuna, sardines, cooked or raw vegetables, pulses are a meal in themselves or can be a sturdy accompaniment to fish or frittate Mariuccia-style. No description of the food of the South is complete without recipes which honour this elemental, rustic ingredient.

MARIUCCIA'S LENTILS (INSALATA DI LENTICCHIE)

a quantity of brown or green lentils boiled until tender
1 onion cut vertically into thin slices
4 vine tomatoes cut horizontally into halves and then quarters or a dozen cherry tomatoes cut vertically in halves

1 garlic clove minced
1 red chilli chopped (depending on taste)
a handful of mixed chopped herbs

Mix all the ingredients together in a large bowl.

Add salt and pepper.

Dress with a splash of red balsamic vinegar and a glug of the finest olive oil, then serve.

For extra protein add a fried egg or fried fish with maybe some greens on the side.

CHICKPEA SALAD WITH BLACK OLIVES, GREEN BEANS AND LEMONS (INSALATA DI CECI CON OLIVE, FAGIOLI E LIMONE)

400–600g cooked chickpeas
  (I find the jarred variety larger and more tasty;
  if cooking your own, soak overnight before boiling)
150g of cooked green beans cut on the slant
1 onion sliced thinly
12 cherry tomatoes cut vertically
1 large potato boiled and cubed
6 black olives halved
grated lemon rind
salt and pepper

Mix all the ingredients together in a large bowl.

Season and dress with olive oil and a splash of white balsamic vinegar.

Tinned anchovies would be a good replacement for black olives.

BEAN AND TUNA SALAD WITH CAPERS
(INSALATA DI FAGIOLI CON TONNO E CAPERI)

400–600g cooked or tinned white or borlotti beans, drained (if cooking kidney beans boil for at least 10 minutes to destroy the toxin)
1 red onion finely sliced
a bunch of chives chopped
torn basil leaves
a handful of capers
1 small tin of tuna preserved in olive oil
1 red pepper, chopped
juice of half a lemon
olive oil

Mix all the dry ingredients together and season to taste; add the olive oil, and lemon juice, scatter the basil before serving.

BUTTER BEAN SALAD WITH ROCKET AND BEEF TOMATOES
(FAGIOLI BIANCHI CON RUCOLA E POMODORO)

This is a fragrant, lighthearted dish with none of the earthiness of borlotti and other beans. I generally use tinned butter beans since they are convenient and easier to work with.

2 tins butter beans
a few torn basil leaves
a handful of chives chopped
2 large tomatoes sliced thinly and horizontally
juice of half a lemon
olive oil
salt and pepper

Combine the beans, herbs and tomatoes. Add the juice of half a lemon and olive oil and season to taste.

BEAN STEW (FAGIOLI ALL'UCCELLETTO)

Cannellini beans are traditional in this dish from Tuscany but any beans will do. In some parts of Italy the dish is based on green beans rather than cannellini. All are delicious.

2 tins cannellini beans
250g passata
1 garlic clove chopped
half an onion finely chopped
1 leek finely chopped
olive oil
a handful of sage leaves chopped

In a wide saucepan fry the onion until golden, then add the garlic and chopped leek.

If using green beans cook them in water and set aside.

When the onions, leeks and garlic have completely broken down, add the passata and the liquid from one of the tins of beans.

Bring everything up to a boil and then add the drained beans or the cooked green beans.

Bring to the boil again, then reduce the heat. Add the sage, cover the pan and cook the beans over a low heat for about 20 minutes or until the beans and sauce have combined.

BUTTER BEAN CASSEROLE (FAGIOLI BIANCHI AL FORNO)

1 large carrot roughly chopped
2 stalks celery chopped together with the leaves
3 cloves garlic chopped
1 red pepper and 1 green pepper cut into strips
a handful of dried oregano
2 tins of butter beans (or the equivalent of dried beans soaked overnight and cooked; reserve 1 cup of the cooking water)
250g of passata
juice of half a lemon
olive oil
1 tsp smoked paprika
1 red chilli finely chopped

In an ovenproof dish with a lid, pour enough olive oil to cover the bottom.

Sauté vegetables, chilli and garlic until they start to soften.

Add the beans and the liquid from one tin of beans (or a cupful of the cooking liquid).

Add the passata, the oregano and the paprika.

With a wooden spoon mix the contents of the pan and turn up the heat to high.

Let everything bubble for a few minutes then remove the pan from the stove top. Cover with the lid and place the pan in a preheated oven at 200°C.

After half an hour check and keep checking until the contents of the pan have reduced and the dish resembles a stew.

Sprinkle with lemon juice, herbs that you like and maybe some grated lemon peel.

Serve while hot and still bubbling with a green salad.

SAUTÉED GREENS
(CICORIA, CAVOLO NERO, SPINACI RIPASSATI)

1 onion very finely sliced
spring greens: savoy cabbage, kale, cavolo nero, spinach, pak choi in whatever combination suits you – rainbow swiss chard adds wondrous colour (note: organic is best and any hard stalks as in swiss chard and cavolo nero need to be separated from the leaves and finely chopped)
1 garlic clove finely minced
olive oil
1 red chilli, chopped (optional)

Blanch the green leaves.

Heat the olive oil and fry the garlic, chilli (if using), onion and the finely chopped stalks.

Add the greens, season well and keep turning them over so that they pick up all the flavours. Sometimes I add a little water and keep turning until it has evaporated.

Serve straight from the pan.

This dish is delicious served warm or cold. No one will ever need to be persuaded to 'eat their greens' again!

ROASTED FENNEL (FINOCCHIO AL FORNO)

Such a simple dish but a show stopper, when the vegetables are cooked almost whole and served up golden and sizzling with olive oil. It works beautifully as a side dish or as a follow-up to pasta as a main course.

As an extra layer of flavour, you may want to add grated cheese, parmesan or pecorino (feta would work well) towards the end of the roasting time.

olive oil
3–4 bulbs of fennel
seasoning
grated parmesan or pecorino (optional)

Smear a deep, rectangular, ovenproof dish with olive oil.

Trim the stalks of each fennel bulb.

Cut each fennel bulb vertically into 3 pieces ensuring that each section still holds together.

Lay vertically side by side in the dish.

Pour a little more olive oil over them and roast at 220°C for about 30 minutes, until cooked through.

Fried sage as an addition is delicious.

BRUSSELS SPROUTS WITH PANCETTA (CAVOLETTI DI BRUXELLES O BROCCOLETTI CON AGLIO E PANCETTA)

Brussels sprouts are delicious cooked and then refried with garlic and pancetta. The combination will cure any sprout phobics of their malaise. For the best outcome use...

150g of cubed pancetta
1 garlic clove
a quantity of cooked Brussels sprouts cut in half horizontally
1 tbsp of olive oil

Fry the pancetta then add the garlic.

Add the olive oil.

When the garlic is changing colour, add the greens.

Keep turning them over in the pan and just before serving, take a fork and lightly squash the ingredients down into the pan juices.

For overkill, though there is already a lot of strong flavours, you may want to sprinkle some grated parmesan over the vegetables before bringing to the table.

Another option is to replace the pancetta with toasted walnuts added just before adding the vegetables. Plus gnocchi… to make a complete meal, I often add panfried gnocchi which is a crunchy, robust and delicious addition to any green vegetable/pancetta/garlic combo:

Fry the pancetta and then add the garlic.
Add the olive oil.
When the garlic has changed colour, add a good handful of gnocchi.
Add the cooked greens.

Dressings

OLIVE OIL DRESSINGS

For an olive oil and vinegar dressing, I usually finish my salad by first seasoning with salt and pepper, then adding about a tablespoon or even two, of the best extra virgin olive oil I can afford and I add just a splash of vinegar or lemon juice.

HERB INFUSED OLIVE OIL

Herbs such as parsley, mint, oregano, sage and marjoram all create wonderful herby olive oils that can be served alongside any meat or fish dish or as a topping to a vegetarian casserole, soft polenta, polenta chips or risotto.

Tear the leaves from the stems of the herbs. Grind them together with a few grains of rock salt and a splash of olive oil until the leaves have broken down. Add enough olive oil to make a dressing.

GREMOLATA

Gremolata is a delicious dressing made up of a finely chopped mix of sage, chives, parsley, marjoram and mint or whatever herbs you fancy; mixed with a finely chopped clove of garlic and lemon juice. Mix these finely chopped ingredients (do not use a mixer) into a bowl containing a quantity of olive oil and the juice of a quarter of a lemon or more according to your taste. Add salt and pepper and mix again. The gremolata should look green and the herbs should dominate.

> Tip: How much olive oil and vinegar to use is a matter of taste. However food, and especially salad, must have been touched by the oil but never drenched. Vinegar or lemon juice adds a little acidity but again must be used in a very small quantity. Sometimes, I even omit the vinegar and if well seasoned with salt and pepper, I just enjoy the olive oil.

Gremolata is delicious with fish and seafood. But a tablespoon or two can also be added on to any of the above dishes and salads. Or you can just tear a piece of bread or focaccia in half and dip. Nothing more is really needed as the bread soaks up the tastes and aromas of herbs and the garlicky, fruity olive oil.

PEPPERONCINO

Pepperoncino is a fiery dip which is very popular in Italy. It consists of tinned finely chopped tomatoes, half a finely chopped red pepper and half of a yellow one, a teaspoon of sugar, 1 red chilli chopped very finely, 3 or 4 chopped spring onions, olive oil and salt. A pinch of cumin and ginger can add another layer of heat and depth, if desired. Either mix by hand or place in a food mixer for a few seconds... just enough to break down some, but not all, of the solids.

AGRODOLCE

Agrodolce is a sweet and sour sauce said to be of Arab origin and is therefore to be found more readily in Sicily and southern Italy where it is sometimes added to pasta dishes or as a topping for grilled meat or fish. It is made up of tomato purée, sugar or honey, water, white balsamic vinegar and 1 or 2 chilli peppers. Cooked potatoes are sometimes mashed and added to give a little extra body to this much favoured dressing.

PANGRATTATO

Pangrattato is very much in the tradition of *la cucina povera* since it is said to have come from a time when mainly in the South, people grated stale bread to put over their pasta because they could not afford cheese. The basic recipe is stale bread, olive oil, salt and garlic. Grate the bread until you have rough, largish breadcrumbs and fry in olive oil together with finely chopped garlic. To this, you may want to add some chopped walnuts, pine nuts or almonds; and perhaps some finely chopped chilli or a chopped anchovy. Lemon juice or herbs may also be added at the end.

And to Drink

Again, a crisp, light Corvo Bianco Duca di Salaparuta from Sicily. If red is your preference, a Corvo Rosso, a Nero d'Avola, Primitivo or a medium weight Frappato. All are excellent choices.

The sweet South

Music

'I' te Vurría Vasa' sung by Massimo Ranieri
Napoli A Modo Mio, 2010

'Meridionale' sung by Kalàscima
S Maria Del Fioggiaro, 2010

THERE IS SOMETHING solid and reassuring about a Sunday in the villages and small towns of southern Italy. In Cassino or Lecce, and elsewhere, Sunday has its own smell and feel. Early waking to skies of promise and wellbeing for this day, and maybe hope for every day. The sky at 6am is clear, the air is cool, the land is in gentle harmony… hens scurrying and scratching in the backyard; birdsong, insects buzzing and chattering; and the smell of something tasty in kitchens across the countryside and in the streets. When I am there, Sunday is the best day of the week and all the better, all the simpler, all the more direct an experience, the further south I go.

La domenica is still a day of celebration in many homes across Italy. It is a day when the world fades; peace settles; the entire place takes a breath; reverts to its essence; becomes itself. I am no longer a churchgoer, but I still love church bells, the tradition and reliability of a Sunday in Italy. The message across the vast, still landscapes, *la pianura* and mountains, and posted on social media from friends in Viticuso, Casalvieri and elsewhere in my Italy, is a wish for *una giornata tranquilla* (a peaceful day); *un giorno di riposo* or day of rest. Sunday is a day of reunions, of meeting with loved ones. A day of kinship and old friendships, inter-generational mixing and warm exchange.

Sunday is about a strong arm and care for the hardy elderly; about children in their Sunday shoes, lacy socks, dressed to impress. Clean-shaven old men, worn down by sun and a life's toil, in crisp white shirts and maybe a light jacket. Women in their best, artfully preserved and freshly laundered cottons and silks, maybe from a 'bottom drawer' decades since, smelling of fresh soap and cologne. *La domenica* is a hallowed day of gatherings outside churches, of body hugs and men warmly kissing *il buongiorno* (it is a wonderful sight to see men kiss and cry). It is gangs of older women and earthy laughter (for these women know a thing or two); of proud new fathers, shy girls, and bragging young boys.

Gatherings too, outside the local bar. And Sunday may even be a day, just this one day, when those older, world-savvy women might accept a cheeky *amaro* or a vermouth before setting off up the road to prepare for the arrival of family and feasting.

On this day for certain, shops are closed – all, that is, except for sellers of flowers, of chocolate, and *pasticcerie*, where you will drop in on the way to lunch, in order to pick up a gift before your day's visit.

The sun of the South is a constant presence that you work with. Your day revolves around its strength and you adapt your daily pace and timetable to its will and cycle. Lunch is generally eaten in the cool of indoors: table noise of clatter, of voices, of cadenced shouts of delight, surprise, encouragement… '*su mamma su*' (come on, eat it up!) gently fade into the late afternoon. And such is the weight of the day's heat that the streets are now heavy with quiet. There is only the now quietened hum of table chat, a few after-feast lingerers. Most people are asleep having dozed off; older relations have taken to their beds and there is no one to be seen in the streets, except maybe, a stray, wandering tourist, peering at ancient walls while pulling on her sun hat.

In the same way that southern Italian Sunday mornings are memorable, there is a distinctiveness about Sunday evenings and nights. The same solidity and reassurance of morning time applies to nightfall. You will walk the pavements of Polignano a Mare in Puglia, Ballarò market in Palermo, Piazza Duomo in Ravello and the Jewish ghetto of Testaccio in Rome with the same assurance that all is well in the world. In these streets you walk without a care, because of the people – the families, the prams, the fresh, impatient strutting boys and girls, couples on park benches and the old and all-seeing, watching the world with a smile. And because Italians take their rest in the afternoon, they are people of the night, and night-time goes on and on.

Any lover of life, any seeker of excitement and adventure,

cannot fail to appreciate the energy and contentedness of a Sunday evening. As sun and heat recede and coolness descends, shops open and pace, verve and voices rise. In Bari, Viareggio and the seaside resorts of *le cinque terre,* a Sunday evening is all jostle, bustle and very often, in tourist resorts, brisk business. It is large store bags and shopping, outrageously bejewelled sandals, oversized bling (or the real thing). It is singly, or in twos or threes, women with hands of experience, with practised eye and hand, appraising the crispest cotton, the finest weaves. And Sunday evening is impatient, assured children and the sound of shrieking at mischievous sons on runaway cycles. It is the air-filled humming pleasure from all around, at joyful children and carefully turned-out tots. All of these delights will make you turn, stop and stare. They will fill your eyes with wonder and good-humoured laughter, will make your heart beat faster and propel you on with a new energy, to face the next few months and years, in your settled day-to-day at home, in northern cold and grey skies and cities. All of these experiences represent much, much more than a holiday. They are both a profound meditation and an invitation to live better, to live more fully and creatively, to dwell in the present and to be open, always, to the new.

What distinguishes Sunday nights mostly, besides late night pizzas, at best eaten in Frascati just above Rome for instance, is *gelato*. There is no greater social mix and equaliser than an Italian *gelateria artigianale* (a homemade ice cream shop) Like *pizzerie* everywhere, there is no more interesting a crowd either, than the queue outside. Young fathers emerge mob-handed with a clutch of cones for their waiting families, and for many, maybe the weekly treat. They rub shoulders with expansive older men, strangely childlike, licking a cone; with fair-haired Americans, in shorts, excited at the transition from an ordinary ice cream to the mystique of a *gelato*; with backpackers counting their euros blocking the doorway; and solitary well-coiffed and quality-dressed middle-aged women having a sly treat after a day in the kitchen.

Apart from ice cream – which is a treat families take to the street for, emerging in family groups after a long, luxurious day at home – Italians don't really do puddings. Or if they do, one has the sense that they are an add-on, an import. I certainly find them an imposition. I usually leave my dessert planning until the last minute and then conveniently run out of time. I recently mentioned this Italian disinterest in matters sweet to a Scottish friend who has spent several years in Italy. I was sorely discomfited though by her look of surprise: 'what about *torta della nonna?*' she exclaimed. Neither my Grandma or any other *nonna* I have met, for whom meals are about nourishment and necessity, has ever made a torta. My confidence was thankfully restored by Hazan, author of many books on Italian food; the doyenne of Italian cookery, an inspiration for generations of both home and professional cooks. She writes:

> It is likely that even the most enterprising Italian cook will bake no more than one cake or a batch of biscuits in a year... nor would it be surprising, if in a lifetime of cooking she produced nothing more elaborate for dessert than a bowl of fruit.

The delights of tiramisù, zabaglione and panna cotta are the domain of treats, festivals, restaurants and professionals. We home cooks, *per fortuna* (thankfully) are ever free to do what we know and love to cook best.

In most Italian homes I have been in, apart from the practice of soaking sticky peaches, flesh exposed and lush, in a glass of wine for hours, fruit, and in particular small sweet pears, is served after the meal, most often with cheese. While the thought of this in Britain may not excite in the way that a pistachio and chocolate soufflé does, when compared to the soft, sweetness of fresh fruit from a bountiful southern Italian orchard, steps from your front door, awash with daily sunshine, there is surely no competition. And I am very sure too, that given the choice, a southern Italian would opt for fruit rather than any heavily sugared treat.

Although not big on desserts, southern Italy, indeed Italy in general, has a wonderful tradition of sweetened fried dough, made with flour, eggs, butter or olive oil and sugar (if making sweet pastries). Each family has its own recipe and its own word for these: *sciaun'*, *sciusc'*e or *crustol'e*. The dough is rolled out and shaped according to custom, fried and served as an appetiser and something to have with pre-lunch drinks. Savoury versions stuffed with cheese, pancetta or sausage meat are served at Easter and Christmas.

The famous and now ubiquitous tiramisù dessert originates from the Venice area of Italy. Done well and fresh, it is a lovely soft, alcohol-infused cushion which requires little effort other than lifting the spoon to one's mouth. I have made it and served it many times. But true to my own heritage, with the exception of the odd tiramisù, I like to serve a homemade ricotta after a meal. Homemade ricotta, sturdier and more delicate in flavour than bought versions, is delicious, especially when drizzled with a quality Italian honey, fresh hazelnuts on the side.

HOMEMADE RICOTTA (RICOTTA FRESCA)

For this you need a sieve or a ricotta mould and a bowl big enough to accommodate it.

1 litre of milk
juice of half a lemon

Bring the milk to a rolling boil and pour in the lemon juice. The mixture will start to break into flakes.

Mix it well with a wooden spoon.

Turn off the heat and cover the saucepan for at least 10 minutes.

Position the mould inside a bowl and empty the mix into it.

Carefully lift out the mould containing the ricotta. Turn it upside down and empty the cheese onto a serving dish. Cover it loosely with foil and put in the fridge for 2 or 3 hours, the longer the better.

> Tip: To avoid your cheese becoming too dry, let the mixture in the mould sit for a while in its own juices. Gather some of the liquid and pour it through the cheese again.

And to Drink

There is no better whisky than the dazzling array from the Scottish islands of Islay and Jura. Among my favourites are Laphraiog, Lagavulin, Bruichladdich and Jura malt. These represent the glories of the peat; of the clear, rushing waters and mizzle or low-hanging mists of one of the most beautiful parts of our planet. Think firesides, shawls, tales of ghouls, heroes, heritage and culture.

Grappa is Italy's equivalent. Produced mainly in the northern regions, grappa is made from the pips and skins left over from the vinification process. The Marsala region of Sicily has only recently obtained official recognition for its local grappa. Grappa Dell' Etna and Grappa di Nero d'Avola are very well worth trying accompanied by a full-bodied, aromatic caffè espresso.

Arancello, another option, well worth trying and a welcome alternative to the ubiquitous limoncello, is a liqueur made from bitter oranges around the Amalfi coast.

A particular way of life

Music

*'Cavatina' by Giovanni Paisiello
from The Barber of Seville (YouTube)*

VITICUSO, LIKE MOST villages in the South of Italy and elsewhere, has a patron saint. St Anthony (Sant' Antonin) who died a martyr in Syria in the Middle Ages is honoured every year on the 1st of September, a feast day for which those who have left the village to live elsewhere return in droves. For some, the gathering, which lasts several days, is ostensibly a religious festival. But most people gather there, returning from countries all over the world, to come and to stand together as a community, to meet friends, and enjoy family. Pop up eateries and makeshift stalls showcase the best of local produce; of local skills, flair and creativity and back-breaking endeavour. As one, young and old unite to honour their, at times, savage history. They come together to celebrate their roots in the land that endowed them with the wherewithal to remain and to thrive there; or the talent and skill to establish themselves and make their mark in a wider world where as strangers, they often had to think on their feet in response to changing fortunes.

Towns and cities in the South of Italy are often criticised for their 'unproductive' economy and slow lifestyle. A way of life which clings to the past. Italian politics are full of polemics and fierce debate about the problems of the South which are real and pressing, particularly in the wake of the pandemic. But as the decades turn, we find ourselves as a society, increasingly challenged by world events, those lifestyles and values on which the modern world has been built, under closer scrutiny. It seems that in order to go forward, we have begun to grasp perhaps, the urgency of looking backwards, to research, to recover, to recycle and to relearn old ways.

This book is a series of snapshots and evocations of a particular culture which is still alive today... in Viticuso, Picinisco, all the hamlets up and down the southern lands of a country that I am honoured to call mine, and which, I believe, has much to teach us. The culture of this still unsung land has much to offer our current times. Respect and love of nature and the land; delight in a rich harvest, in neighbours, in holding a grandchild; in the aroma of rising dough; in racing clouds, in the blessed rain, in the sun of early rising; in birdsong, working bees, and flowering shrubs and trees. Most importantly, an expression of that delight and joy through long lazy hours and days spent with intimates and loved ones at a generous table put together with a pure and open heart.

I have spent many years as someone from an immigrant family, trying very hard in many areas of my life, and very often, not too successfully, to 'fit'. As the months of the pandemic passed, those layers fell away. I felt a new hunger for truth, a need to embrace a part of me that I had tried to hide and to ignore.

Magnaccioni: My Food… My Italy celebrates arrival and it celebrates otherness and difference. It celebrates a precious birthright and legacy. It is a joyful recognition of what has been gifted to me… a particular set of values that I am privileged to have grown up with and that I hope I have laid down for my daughters and those who follow them.

It occurred to me only recently that, as I wrote this book, I gradually shifted from writing about 'other' to writing about what is as much mine to own.

It is then, with great pride and much pleasure that I share it with you.

The food

artichokes
 sautéed with garlic and lemons (carciofi trifolati) 60

beans
 bean stew (fagioli all'uccelletto) 161
 butter bean casserole (fagioli bianchi al forno) 162
 bean and tuna salad with capers (insalata di fagioli con tonno e caperi) 160
 butter bean salad with rocket and beef tomatoes (fagioli bianchi con rucola e pomodoro) 160

bread
 crostini, canapés based on small rounds of toasted bread (crostini semplici) 90
 focaccia 41
 pangrattato 167
 piadine (Italian flatbreads) 43

broccoli
 broccoli fritters (frittelle di broccoli) 62

cauliflower
 with olives and lemons (cavolfiore con olive e limone) 52
 with tuna (cavolfiore con tonno) 53

dressings
 agrodolce 167

eggs
 uova al sugo di pomodoro 127

fennel
 roasted (finocchio al forno) 163

fish
 fish soup (zuppa di pesci) 149
 fritto misto 30
 smoked haddock Italian style (pesce scozzese) 56

frittate
 Easter (frittata pasqualina) 81
 leftover pasta (frittata di pasta) 76
 mozza (frittata con mozzarella) 78
 Savoy cabbage, onion and potato (frittata con verza, cipollo e patate) 75
 simple (frittata di terra) 74

mushrooms
 mushrooms with lemons and walnuts (funghi con noci e limone) 51

pasta
 orzo with pesto and hazelnuts (orzo al pesto con nocciole) 116
 pasta and bean stew Viticuso style (pasta e fagiol' alla viticusar) 113
 pasta, preparing 99
 pastina (small pasta for soup) 123
 spaghetti with a garlic and olive oil sauce (spaghetti all'aglio e olio) 116
 shells, stuffed (conchiglioni ripieni) 110
 soffritto 106
 trofie with pesto (trofie al pesto genovese) 108
 trofie with potatoes and green beans (trofie con patate e fagiolini) 109

pesto
 pesto (pesto di basilico)

polenta
 polenta, classic (polenta al sugo di pomodoro) 141
 scagliozzi (street food of the south) 142

pulses
 lentils, Mariuccia's (insalata di lenticchie) 158

ragù
  ragù di salsiccia 103

ricotta
  ricotta, homemade (ricotta fresca) 160

risotto
  aubergines, basil and feta (risotto alle melanzane con basilico e feta) 137
  beetroot, mint and goats cheese (risotto alla barbietola con formaggio di capra) 138

  mushrooms and black olives (risotto alla romana) 135
  smoked haddock and peas (risotto di pesci e piselli) 134

salad
  bread salad (panzanella) 157
  brussels sprouts with pancetta (cavoletti di Bruxelles o broccoletti con aglio e pancetta) 164
  chickpea salad with black olives, green beans and lemons (insalata di ceci con olive, fagioli e limone) 159
  potato salad (insalata di patate) 54
  sautéed greens (cicoria, cavolo nero, spinaci ripassati) 163
  tomato and onion salad (insalata di pomodori) 45

sauces
  béchamel 112
  beef (ragù napoletano or ragù di manzo) 101
  bolognese 111
  gremolata 166
  pepperoncino 166
  tomato sauce, light (sugo di pomodori freschi) 104
  tomato sauce, medium to rich (sugo di pomodori) 105

soup
  fish soup (zuppa di pesci) 149
  minestrone (la minestra) 128
  minestrone, green (minestrone alla ligure) 129
  pappa or pappocce' 130
  pastina in a broth (pastina in brodo) 124
  stracciatella 124

stew
  picchiapò 126

stock
  beef 122
  chicken 122
  vegetable 121

tomatoes
  beef tomatoes, stuffed (pomodori ripieni) 47
  tomatoes, marinaded (pomodori all'aglio) 45

The wine

whites
Arneis (Piemonte)
Bombino Bianco (Puglia)
Chardonnay (Puglia)
Corvo Bianco (Sicily)
Falanghina (Campania)
Fiano (Campania)
Frascati (Lazio)
Garganega (Veneto)
Pecorino (Abruzzi)
Vermentino Di Sardegna (Sardegna)
Greco Di Tufo (Campania)

reds
Amarone (Veneto)
Aleatico (Lazio)
Cesanese del Piglio (Lazio)
Corvo Rosso (Sicily)
Frappato (Sicily)
Nero d'Avola (Sicily)
Primitivo (Puglia)
Nero Di Troia (Puglia)
Bombino Nero (Puglia)
Montepulciano (Abruzzi)

vermouth and aperitivi
Aperol
Cacc'e Mmitte di Lucera (Sardinia)
Orvieto Classico Abboccato (Tuscany)
Negroni

grappe
Grappa Dell' Etna
Grappa di Nero D'Avola

The music

Magnaccioni

Anne Pia's *Magnaccioni* playlist can be found at: open.spotify.com/playlist/4E48DLkWoixXJnLu2ylZJd?si=LX-FQEn5TRO8tr-HD2FSDg

A place to start

'Vitti 'na Crozza': Sicilian song sung by Antonio Castrignanò (b. 1977) from Salento in Puglia.
youtube.com/watch?v=sZPn2Kb5SQo

'La Societá dei Magnaccioni': sung in Roman by Lando Fiorini (1938–2017), born and died in Rome.
youtube.com/watch?v=liuApR7oLz8

'Com'e facette mammeta?': sung in Neapolitan by Massimo Ranieri (b. 1951, Naples).
youtube.com/watch?v=KwEgNA2Rv_U

Antipasti... relaxing with guests

'Terra straniera' sung in Italian by Beniamino Gigli (1890–1957), born and died in Rome.
youtube.com/watch?v=q5u2flcQqjE

'Passione' sung in Neapolitan by Freddie de Tommaso (b. 1924 in the UK); his father was from Puglia.
youtube.com/watch?v=WIdRcQUrJII

Le frittate

'The Dark Town Strutters Ball' (Italian style): sung in Laziali/Calabrese by Lou Monte (Louis Scaglione) (1917–89), an American Italian of Calabrian descent.
youtube.com/watch?v=g1Ouw3ibXmY

'Parlami d'amore Mariú': sung in Italian by Mario Lanza (1921–1959), born in the USA, of Filignano, Abruzzi origin.
youtube/hOLOroK7Q1Y

L'ora dell'aperitivo

'E lucevan le stelle': aria from the Puccini opera, *Tosca*, sung in Italian by Enrico Caruso (1873–1921), born and died in Naples.
youtube.com/watch?v=3TjEoAXzJ9E

Allegro from the 'Mandolin Concerto in G Major' by Domenico Gaudioso; Neapolitan, 18th century.
youtube.com/watch?v=KVd4HZ9KrXo

The best of life

'Tammuriata Nera': sung in Neapolitan by the Nuova Compagnia di Canto Popolare.
youtube.com/watch?v=gkTyRvYoEUI

'A' Finestra'
Sung in Sicilian by Carmen Console (b. 1974).
youtube.com/watch?v=dvV8TaLOV-Y

Aria Io vi amo... Deliro, ti amo sono pazzo from the opera *Cyrano de Bergerac* composed by Franco Alfano (1875–1954); born in Posillipo, Naples region.
youtube.com/watch?v=FayZ63koKJ8

La cucina povera

'Viva la pappa col pomodoro': sung in Italian by Italian-Swiss singer Rita Pavone (b. 1945)
youtube.com/watch?v=kgC2D-bvUKE

'A pizza': sung in Neapolitan by Aurelio Fierro (1923–2005) from Avellino, Campania.
youtube.com/watch?v=8YNbqKsC2xs

Ports, boats and Marechiaro

'Marechiare': sung in Neapolitan by Claudio Villa (1926–87), born in Trastevere, Rome.
youtube.com/watch?v=thmz2_W-wqQ

'Chiaro di luna': sung in Italian by Italian singer-songwriter and rapper Lorenzo Cherubini, known as Jovanotti (b. 1966, Rome).
youtube.com/watch?v=Ro8PdDjKA3o

La cucina di terra

'La canzone del pane': sung by I Camillas; rock group from Pesaro. Active from 2004 to 2020.
youtube.com/watch?v=famtpC7t23o

Ciaccona by Francesca Caccini (1587–1640), born in Florence. An Italian composer, singer, lutenist, poet and music teacher of the early Baroque era.
youtube.com/watch?v=bIYvV4CIAow

The sweet South

'I te vurria vasà': sung by Freddie de Tommaso (b. 1924 in the UK); his father was from Puglia.
youtube.com/watch?v=6b46Lcdg2PY

'Meridionale': sung by Kalascima, one of Italy's hottest bands, six friends from Salento celebrating the culture of Italy's South.
youtube.com/watch?v=LzhzppPIXPk

A particular way of life

'Cavatina (Saper Bramate)' from *The Barber of Seville*, a comic opera by Giovanni Paisiello (1740–1816), born in Roccaforzata, Puglia.
youtube.com/watch?v=aoHC5Y-oRqU

'Aria Il Mio Ben Quando Verrà' from Paisiello's comic opera *Nina, o sia la Pazza per Amore:* sung by Cecilia Bartoli (1966—); born in Rome and studied at the Conservatorio di Santa Cecilia, Roma.(Cav.)

The language

alla giudìa	Jewish style
alla romana	Roman style
alta moda	high fashion
antipasto	small appetisers
asado (Sp)	an array of barbecued meat found in Argentina
baccalà	dried salt cod
ballarella	traditional dance of the ciociaria
battiporte	door knocker
barbietola	beetroot
un boccone	a mouthful
broccolini	baby broccoli
brodo	broth
bruschette	toasted bread-based appetisers
il buongiorno	a greeting; dire il buongiorno to say hello
burrata	a soft cheese made from mozzarella
caciocavallo	a cheese in Southern Italy, the curd is from sheep or cow's milk and shaped like a teardrop
cacio e pepe	is made with pepper and caciocavallo
caffè corretto	espresso coffee with a drop of alcohol
campanilismoa	term used in Italy meaning identity not defined by the country of origin, but by village, region or culture
c'ert'e bafagn'e re call'	so much heat!
gl'chioghere	traditional footwear, clogs; worn in the villages in the South
cime di rapa	turnip greens
la ciociaria	a historically, socially deprived area of villages around Rome
con cuore	hearty, heartfelt
colla pomarol' n' goppe	with tomato on top
cornetto con crema	horn-shaped pastry filled with crema pasticcera corniccione outer crust of a pizza
cortaderia (Sp)	pampas grasses of South America
cortile	Italian courtyard, cloister sometimes vaulted
cotechino	Italian large pork sausage cooked slowly
cotoletta alla milanese	veal fried in breadcrumbs
crema di pepperoncino	dipping sauce or spice made of chilli peppers, olive oil, garlic and salt
crespelle	light, savoury Italian pancakes stuffed and baked
crostini	canapés based on small rounds of toasted bread
la cucina povera	simple, peasant fare
la cucina romanesca	Roman cooking
la cucina di terra	local food from the land

THE LANGUAGE

donne di casa	women working in the home
farinata (pl. e)	a thin pizza made with chickpea flour (gram flour) and water
fettuccine	ribbon shaped pasta typical of Rome
focaccia	a flat olive oil bread, usually square (focaccia al bianco no tomatoes)
formaggi	cheeses
friselle	small round of rough bread, twice baked and common in the South of Italy, mainly Puglia
frittelle	deep fried rounds of dough, used in Puglia for dipping or stuffing
fritto misto	mixed seafood, fish and vegetables in batter fried
gelaterie artigianali	shops selling their own homemade ice cream
genio casalinga	the skill and genius of home cooks
gl'pisciadur'	chamber pot
gle zampogne	double chantered bagpipes, traditional in the South
gremolata	dipping sauce made of finely chopped herbs, garlic, olive oil and lemon
guanciale	cured pork meat made from pork cheeks
huevos rancheros (Sp)	ranch style eggs, cooked in a spicy tomato sauce; typical Mexican breakfast.
ingredienti semplici	simple ingredients; ingredienti di scarti; using leftovers; ingredienti pregiati; fine, high cost ingredients
insaladone	a hearty salad
insalata di broccoli	broccoli salad
una giornata tranquilla	a peaceful day
un giorno di ripsoso	a day of rest
lazialo (laziali)	adj. meaning from Lazio
la madonna	the Virgin Mary
maison de campagne (Fr)	country house
mangiamaccheroni	a slightly derogatory term for people from the South of Italy 'maccheroni eaters'
magnaccioni	foodies, people who are devoted to good fare
'magne mamm' ca te fa ross'	eat up wee one and grow big and strong
maniere	ways, style, affectations
mantecato	a mix of butter and grated parmesan or pecorino cheese added to a risotto before serving

melanzane alla parmigiana	baked aubergines and parmesan cheese
el mercado central (Sp)	the main market
merenda	mid-morning snack
il Mezzogiorno	the South of Italy
la minestra	a hearty soup
mozzarella in carrozza	a Southern Italian sandwich made from fried cheese (muzzaré the Neapolitan word for mozzarella; mozza' abbreviation)
mortadella	a cured pork meat with grains of black pepper, pistachio or berries
motocicletti	motorcycles
'nduja	a spicy, spreadable pork sausage from Calabria
necessitá fa virtú	necessity is the mother of invention
la ninna nanna	rocking a baby to sleep; lullaby
nonna, mammina, grammi, mimi	a child's words for grandmother
nostr'e part'	our part of Italy, where we come from
olive all'ascolana	once or twice fried stuffed olives
l'ora dell'aperitivo	the aperitive hour
ossobuco	a veal stew from Lombardia; ossobuco alla milanese – veal stew cooked in a beef stock and traditionally served with a milanese risotto
palazzi	large imposing building in Italy
pan con tomate (Sp)	bread and grated tomatoes with olive oil and salt
panini	a small loaf, usually round or oval, filled with meat or cheese
pan casarau	traditional flatbread from Sardinia
pane casereccio	long, small sandwich bread made with wheat bran, flour and natural yeast.
panzanella	salad based on yesterday's bread
pappa or pappocce	slops made from stale bread
pangrattato	rough breadcrumbs usually fried and used as a topping
pasta e patate	pasta and potatoes
past'e patat'	a dish of pasta with potatoes
pecorino	a table or cooking cheese made from sheep's milk (pecorino romano (from Rome); pecorino sardo (from Sardinia)
pesto	a sauce or dip made from crushed garlic, pine nuts, basil and olive oil
pharmacie (Fr)	chemist
picchiare	to nibble

piccante	spicy
pizza bianche	white pizza… no tomatoes
pizza al taglio	pizza sold by the slice
pizzette	mini pizzas
pollo alla milanese	fried chicken breast in breadcrumbs
polentoni	a slightly derogative term for people from the North of Italy 'polenta eaters'
portone	large, heavy outside door
prosciutto cotto	cooked ham
provolone	a Southern Italian cheese
la questione della lingua	the vexed language issue… what is the language of Italy?
ragù	a meat and tomato-based sauce (d'agnello; lamb based; di manzo; beef based)
riciclare	recycling
risotto alla milanese	saffron based risotto typical of the Milan area
salotto di Milano	Milan's drawing room
saltimbocca	a dish of veal and prosciutto cooked in white wine
salumi	mixed cured meats
scamorza	a Southern Italian cow's milk cheese
soffritto	a mix of chopped onion, carrot and celery or leeks as a base for risottos and pasta sauce)
strozzapreti al pomodoro	small twists of pasta (strangle the priests) in a tomato sauce
su' mamma su'	words of encouragement used for children
tramezzini	British style sandwiches (un'tramesin' Venetian for tramezzino)
trasformare al meglio	to bring out the best
trifolati	fried in olive oil and garlic
un'a me e cent' a te	do one on me and I'll return it a hundred times more
vino rosato	rosé wine
volare	to fly
zuppa di pesci	fish soup made with whole seafood and white fish

Key to family collage (p.10)

Clockwise from top left:
Mum (Cristina Rossi) and me.
My great-grandmother (Cristina Cocozza), Emilio Rossi's mother.
Cristina Rossi.
Grandma (Maria 'Mariuccia' Rossi, née Coletta), 'The Duchess'.
Grandma in Viticuso with relatives.
Auntie Louise (Louisa Coletta, née Rossi), Mum's sister.
My grandparents (Emilio Rossi and Maria 'Mariuccia' Rossi, née Coletta).

Centre:
My girls. Left to right: Sophie-Louise, 4, Camilla, 12 and Roberta, 7.
Grandma in Viticuso with her sister, another Cristina and her cousin Nicandro.

Acknowledgements

Thanks to Sheila McMillan and Siobhan Canavan for helpful comments on early drafts and continual encouragement throughout the process, to Sharon Doherty for road testing some of the recipes and her constant enthusiasm for my food; and to Paul and my girls, Camilla, Roberta and Sophie-Louise for all the joyful food moments and happy family times, particularly in Italy.

Thanks to my friends in Viticuso and surrounding villages for their wonderful welcome last year and for interest in all my endeavours.

Warmest thanks are also due to Jennie Renton my editor, for all the discussions, challenges and time spent, and Madeleine Mankey at Main Point Books. Also thanks to Amy Turnbull of Luath Press for her enthusiastic promotion of this and my other Luath books.

Luath Press Limited

committed to publishing well written books worth reading

LUATH PRESS takes its name from Robert Burns, whose little collie Luath (*Gael.*, swift or nimble) tripped up Jean Armour at a wedding and gave him the chance to speak to the woman who was to be his wife and the abiding love of his life. Burns called one of the 'Twa Dogs' Luath after Cuchullin's hunting dog in Ossian's *Fingal*. Luath Press was established in 1981 in the heart of Burns country, and is now based a few steps up the road from Burns' first lodgings on Edinburgh's Royal Mile. Luath offers you distinctive writing with a hint of unexpected pleasures.
Most bookshops in the UK, the US, Canada, Australia, New Zealand and parts of Europe, either carry our books in stock or can order them for you. To order direct from us, please send a £sterling cheque, postal order, international money order or your credit card details (number, address of cardholder and expiry date) to us at the address below. Please add post and packing as follows: UK – £1.00 per delivery address; overseas surface mail – £2.50 per delivery address; overseas airmail – £3.50 for the first book to each delivery address, plus £1.00 for each additional book by airmail to the same address. If your order is a gift, we will happily enclose your card or message at no extra charge.

Luath Press Limited
543/2 Castlehill
The Royal Mile
Edinburgh EH1 2ND
Scotland
Telephone: 0131 225 4326 (24 hours)
Email: sales@luath.co.uk
Website: www.luath.co.uk

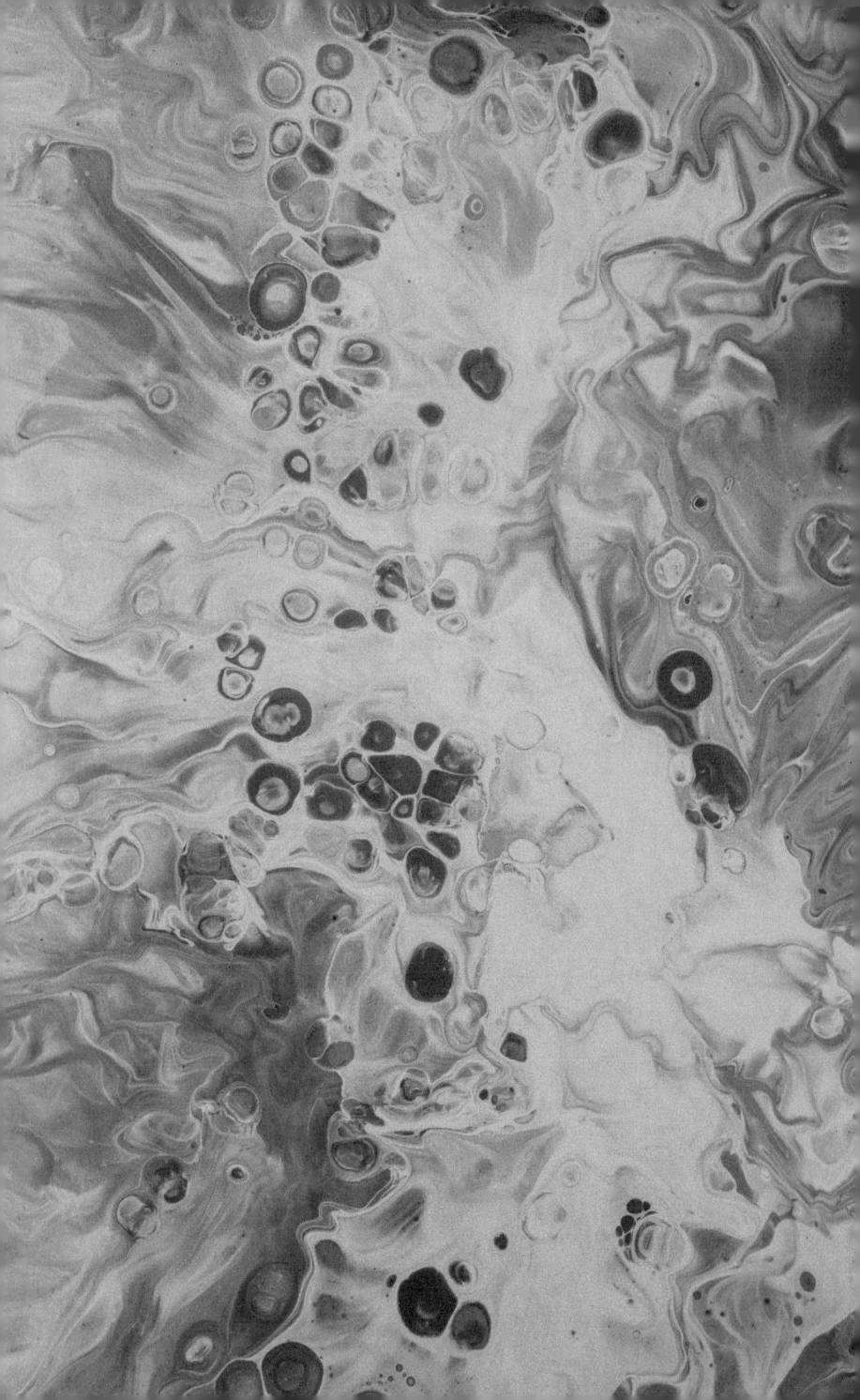